Religion and Politics in Maryland on the Eve of the Civil War:
The Letters of W. Wilkins Davis

Maryland Historical Society, Baltimore

William Wilkins Davis

Religion and Politics in Maryland on the Eve of the Civil War:
The Letters of W. Wilkins Davis

By David Hein

WIPF & STOCK · Eugene, Oregon

Wipf and Stock Publishers
199 W 8th Ave, Suite 3
Eugene, OR 97401

Religion and Politics in Maryland on the Eve of the Civil Wa
The Letters of W. Wilkins Davis
By Hein, David
Copyright©1988 by Hein, David
ISBN 13: 978-1-60608-633-9
Publication date 4/6/2009

Previously published under the title "A Student's View of the
College of St. James on the Eve of the Civil War:
The Letters of W.Wilkins Davis (1842-1866)," and is still av
in hardback from Edwin Mellen Press, 1988.

Contents

List of Illustrations..........................vi
Acknowledgments........................ vii
Note on Editorial Method viii
List of Abbreviations ix

I. The Historical Setting of the Letters........ 1
   The College of St. James................... 3
   Maryland on the Eve of the Civil War 23
   The Episcopal Church in Maryland 32
   The Davis Family 36

II. The Letters of W. Wilkins Davis 55
   Wilkins at Mr. Prentiss's School 55
   Wilkins at the College of St. James 60
   Wilkins's Later Career and Death........ 129

III. Conclusion 143

List of Illustrations

William Wilkins Davis ....frontispiece
William Rollinson Whittingham 4
College of St. James 10
John Barrett Kerfoot...................... 15
Greenwood................................ 37
Greenwood Today 38
Allen Bowie Davis 40
Esther Wilkins Davis...................... 42
Mary Dorsey Davis 43
Hester Ann Wilkins Davis 50
Henry Benjamin Whipple 131

Acknowledgments

The editor of these letters wishes to thank the following persons for their assistance on this project:

F. Garner Ranney, Maryland Diocesan Archives; Jane C. Sween, Montgomery County Historical Society; Jean Haskell, West St. Paul, Minnesota; Robert J. Skarr, Smithsonian Institution Libraries; Francis P. O'Neill, Maryland Historical Society; the Reverend Charles R. McGinley, St. Mark's Church, Lappans, MD; the Reverend Jack S. Scott, St. John's Church, Olney, MD; Arthur Martin, Dorla Shaffer, and Nicole Bissonette, Apple Library, Hood College; Susan Bertram, Department of Education, and Harry St. Ours, Department of Art, Hood College; Jean Baker, Department of History, Goucher College; David Holmes, Department of Religion, College of William and Mary; and John C. Frye, Western Maryland Room, Washington County Free Library.

Note on Editorial Method

The "expanded," rather than the "literal" or the "modernized," method of emendation has been adopted in the redaction of these letters. The editor has followed the author's capitalization and spelling faithfully except that he has capitalized the beginning letter of each sentence and he has expanded some contractions and abbreviations. Superior letters have been brought down to the line of text. Interlineations have also been brought down to the line of text, and cancelled passages have been omitted. Punctuation is preserved as in the original manuscript except that dashes are rendered as commas, dashes, or periods according to their apparent function in the sentence. Editorial comments interpolated in the text are enclosed in square brackets; expanded forms of dates and proper names are printed in roman type and enclosed in square brackets. Omissions made by the editor within a sentence are indicated by suspension points. Nonauthorial emendations have been ignored.

Abbreviations

ABD	Allen Bowie Davis
ABD Letters	Allen Bowie Davis Letters, MS.1511, Maryland Historical Society, Baltimore
ABD Papers	Allen Bowie Davis Papers, MS. 285, Maryland Historical Society
EWD	Esther Wilkins Davis
HAD	Hester Ann Wilkins Davis
HMPEC	*Historical Magazine of the Protestant Episcopal Church*
MDA	Maryland Diocesan Archives, on deposit at the Maryland Historical Society
MDD	Mary Dorsey Davis
MHM	*Maryland Historical Magazine*
MHS	Maryland Historical Society
RDD	Rebecca Dorsey Davis
WWD	William Wilkins Davis

I
The Historical Setting of the Letters

Historians of the Episcopal Church and of American education have long recognized the significance of the College of St. James, established in 1842 near Hagerstown, Maryland. Much has been written about the school's founding, its relationship to earlier endeavors, its trials and unfortunate demise during the Civil War years, and its lasting influence on other institutions, most notably St. Paul's School in Concord, New Hampshire. Indeed, when one combines the impressive secondary literature (especially that which has appeared over the past twenty-five years) with the voluminous primary documents--literary society pamphlets, the correspondence of the principal figures, printed addresses, school registers, and so forth--one finds that one has in view more than enough elements to gain a full picture of the school's purposes, program, and historical import. And yet a consideration of the College of St. James based on these sources alone would lack one thing: a glimpse of the school from the inside provided by the testimony of one who was neither teacher nor trustee nor ecclesiastic. One can possess an adequate knowledge of a school's policies and curriculum, of its founders' intentions and faculty's labors, of its whole external history, and still have very little understanding of its inner life, particularly as experienced by those who were the institution's presumed beneficiaries. Recent historians of the English public schools have enriched their narratives immeasurably by drawing upon the diaries and letters of the boys who endured such places as Eton and Harrow and Westminster and Rugby in the first half of the nineteenth century. Regrettably, materials in such copious quantities as exist for the English publics appear to be lacking for many American schools. In the case of the College of St. James, all that is left by way of an immediate, first-hand student version of events is a batch of letters written by a boy named W. Wilkins Davis, who was born the same year the school began and who died--in Faribault, Minnesota, at the residence of the Right Reverend Henry Benjamin Whipple--only two years after it closed. Young Davis's letters from the College of St. James cover the years 1858 to 1861. They were written to members of his family and do furnish insights into student life at the College and into conditions in Maryland on the eve of the Civil War. More than this, however, they give today's reader a sense of a distinctive life meaningful and affecting in its own right.

It may be helpful before taking up the letters themselves to sketch in their background with some introductory remarks about four topics: the College of St. James itself, the situation in Maryland as the war approached, the Episcopal Church in the 1860s, and the family of

W. Wilkins Davis, especially the father, Allen Bowie Davis. After this overview the letters will be presented along with further comments, interpolated at appropriate points, giving more specific information about each letter's context and references.

The College of St. James

A large part of the purpose of the College of St. James was indicated negatively by Bishop William Rollinson Whittingham (1805-1879) to the school's rector, the Reverend John Barrett Kerfoot (1816-1881), in a letter written several years after the College was founded: "... I am ... anxious that there be no heated evanescent religiosity among the boys, no 'revival' ..., no hasty committal to superficial emotions to be followed by the slow dry rot of hypocrisy and crumbling formalism."[1] The school was, in a sense, a concrete expression of Episcopalian piety, which focused not on instant conversion via emotional experiences but on gradual development as a child of God through participation in the church. St. James's was seen as a place where God could work over time through his ministers and the liturgy to raise up followers for life, a place where soil would be prepared to catch and sustain seeds

---
[1] Whittingham to Kerfoot, 19 January 1846, in William Francis Brand, *Life of William Rollinson Whittingham* (New York, 1883), 1:391.

Reprinted from Brand, *Life of Whittingham*, vol. 1, frontispiece.

William Rollinson Whittingham

that would not wither away but instead bear fruit for years to come.[2] Of course Whittingham may have wanted his friend Kerfoot to be on guard not only against evangelicals but also, closer to home, against tendencies in high church piety to emphasize impressive art and architecture, rites and symbols, as sentimental means of producing a reverential, but transitory, spiritual attitude.[3] There was time, in other words, in a family school such as the College of St. James was intended to be, for the patient training and building up of a boy's character; in this "Christian Household" there was opportunity to achieve more than ephemeral commitment based upon superficial religious feeling.[4]

The idea to start an educational institution that would function as a church family, a Christian home, in which the rector would act as father to a whole community, was not original with Whittingham. The founding of the College of St. James, which was the bishop's "most personal and most cherished project,"[5] was carried out in conscious imitation of

---

[2] James McLachlan makes a similar point in *American Boarding Schools: A Historical Study* (New York, 1970), 141.

[3] See Robert Bruce Mullin, *Episcopal Vision/American Reality: High Church Theology and Social Thought in Evangelical America* (New Haven, 1986), 72-78.

[4] John B. Kerfoot, Circular (proposed) for St. James's Hall, 1841, MDA.

[5] Letter received from F. Garner Ranney, Historiographer of the Diocese of Maryland, 30 November 1985.

the work of William Augustus Muhlenberg (1796-1877) on Long Island, New York. Whittingham acknowledged this direct influence in 1842 when he said, "It is no experiment that our school is to undertake at the risk of injury to the first subjects. A system, the growth of years of study, labor, and experience, is to be transplanted in the full vigor of adult perfection by those who have grown up with [it]...."[6] In fact, as James McLachlan has pointed out, the first piece of literature produced by the College of St. James to describe its program was almost exactly the same as an announcement published shortly before by Muhlenberg's school.[7]

Flushing Institute, which opened in the spring of 1828, and St. Paul's College, which was started eight years later, were designed by Muhlenberg to be, in part, academic environments similar to the Round Hill School near Northampton, Massachusetts. Joseph Green Cogswell (1786-1871) and George Bancroft (1800-1891) had opened this school in 1823 after returning from Europe, where the former had visited and been particularly impressed by the thriving school of Philipp Emanuel von Fellenberg (a disciple of the educational pioneer Johann Heinrich Pestalozzi) at Hofwyl, near Berne, Switzerland. What Cogswell saw at Hofwyl that he soon translated to New England and then passed on to Muhlenberg

---

[6] Whittingham, as quoted in Brand, 1:289.

[7] James McLachlan, ed., "The Civil War Diary of Joseph H. Coit," *MHM* 60 (September 1965): 246 n. 4.

was a school that functioned as a family, in which teachers, acting as surrogate parents, lived and worked in close contact with students, guiding them through a detailed round of daily activities designed to develop their attributes to the fullest--all taking place in a rural setting far removed from the corrupting influences of the cities (in the case of Hofwyl, in magnificent surroundings in the Bernese Alps). The Round Hill School survived for eleven years before succumbing to financial woes, attracting during that period sons of rich merchants and of southern planters and establishing itself as the prototype of American boarding schools. When Muhlenberg began the Flushing Institute he referred to the Round Hill School specifically in his promotional literature; when Round Hill was about to close, Cogswell urged parents to send their boys to Muhlenberg's school, and many did so. Muhlenberg took the model his predecessors had provided and added to the emphasis on parental discipline and intellectual and physical development a rigorous moral and religious life; students at his schools attended chapel services twice daily and thus participated in a spiritual program rooted in the practices of a specific tradition. In the mid-1840s his academic experiment came to a halt, largely because of difficulties in raising funds after the Panic of 1837 and the failure of St. Paul's College to win approval from the New York Regents to grant degrees. But before Muhlenberg laid this work aside to go on to other outstanding causes, it was clear that he had succeeded in building a grammar school and college whose entire plan--from the October-to-July calendar to the prescription of ancient languages as the surest foundation of liberal learning to the familial ethos to the ecclesiastical grounding of the institution --could serve as a blueprint for other church schools all over the country.[8]

A lengthy description of Muhlenberg's school and college is unnecessary at this point because when one looks at the College of St. James one sees, in essence, what Muhlenberg was attempting in New York. Like the Flushing Institute, the College of St. James was an isolated community where teachers and students resided together, the former governing the latter to effect improvements in the boys' moral, religious, and intellectual lives.[9] That there should be such complete congruence between the two schools is not surprising given the

---

[8] McLachlan, *American Boarding Schools*, 105-35; J. Kevin Fox, "The Chapels in the Life and Past of St. Paul's School," *National Association of Episcopal Schools Journal* 1 (Winter 1985): 40-42; Frederic Cook Morehouse, *Some American Churchmen* (Milwaukee, 1892), 125-38; August Heckscher, *St. Paul's: The Life of a New England School* (New York, 1980), 3-7; Alvin W. Skardon, *Church Leader in the Cities: William Augustus Muhlenberg* (Philadelphia, 1971), 48-49, 61-90; Anne Ayres, *The Life and Work of William Augustus Muhlenberg*, 5th ed. (New York, 1894), 60, 79, 87-91, 100-101, 112, 126-27, 131-32, 141; John Frederick Woolverton, "William Augustus Muhlenberg and the Founding of St. Paul's College," *HMPEC* 29 (September 1960): 192-218.

[9] McLachlan, *American Boarding Schools*, 132-33. It should be mentioned, though, that, over time, Kerfoot gave up many of the more annoying rules and traditions that had been transplanted from Muhlenberg's Flushing Institute to the College of St. James. There was gradually a reduction in particular of roll calls and inspections. Joseph H. Coit, "Recollections of Bishop Kerfoot's Life and Work at St. James's, Etc.," in Hall Harrison, *Life of the Right Reverend John Barrett Kerfoot...* (New York, 1886), 1:331.

heavy influence through key individuals of the older school on its successor. Whittingham, a member of the Board of Visitors of St. Paul's College, asked Muhlenberg in 1841 to come to Maryland to head the institution known (until 1844) as St. James's Hall. Muhlenberg did visit the palce the bishop had in mind for the school but was unimpressed--the site lacked the woods and swimming holes he felt necessary for the amusement of active boys, and distressingly little progress had been made on the whole undertaking--so he declined Whittingham's offer. Consequently, not Muhlenberg but John Barrett Kerfoot came to Maryland to serve as St. James's first and only rector.[10] Kerfoot had been chaplain of St. Paul's College and an instructor there of Greek and Latin; more importantly, he had been Muhlenberg's principal assistant. The two had known one another ever since Kerfoot as a child of six had attended Muhlenberg's school in Lancaster, Pennsylvania. When John was nine his father died and he came under the care of Muhlenberg, who brought him with him in 1826 to Long Island, where Kerfoot continued his education as Muhlenberg's protégé.[11] The founder of the Flushing Institute and St. Paul's College was happy to see the success his favorite pupil enjoyed as rector of St. James's. On 31 July 1851, at the laying of the cornerstone for a new building

---

[10] J. Thomas Scharf, *History of Western Maryland* (Philadelphia, 1882), 2:1239; Skardon, 89-90; McLachlan, *American Boarding Schools*, 132; Harrison, 1:46.

[11] Harrison, 1:1-4; Skardon, 88.

Reprinted from Harrison, *Life of Kerfoot*, vol. 1, facing p. 45.

College of St. James

at the Maryland school, Muhlenberg said in his address that he recognized the College of St. James as his own cherished school revived, "the offspring bidding fair to outstrip the sire."[12]

The property that Muhlenberg had viewed with some disdain had been procured for the diocese by Whittingham and a group of interested Episcopalians after considerable effort on their part. The Reverend Theodore B. Lyman, rector of St. John's Church in Hagerstown from 1840 to 1849 and later bishop of North Carolina, had recommended to Bishop Whittingham the purchase, for five thousand dollars, of an estate named Fountain Rock located six miles south of Hagerstown as a desirable location for a diocesan school for boys.[13] The property included the manor house of General Samuel Ringgold (1762-1829), the interiors of which had been planned by Benjamin H. Latrobe, and twenty acres of land. With the aid of Lyman and with the financial assistance of Washington County laymen, the transaction was completed and--after Muhlenberg sent his valued assistant south--the school begun. The first academic session commenced on

---

[12] Muhlenberg, as quoted in Harrison, 1:47.

[13] School authorities assured parents that the school's secluded setting was "very favorable to the good order and moral habits of the students." *Register of the College of St. James ... for the Ninth Session, 1850-51* (Baltimore, 1851), 5.

Monday, 3 October 1842, with fourteen students in attendance.[14]

The College of St. James grew quickly. Starting in the late 1840s the school regularly enrolled over a hundred students a year.[15] While the faculty was largely northern, the students tended to be from all over the South, with the largest group coming from Baltimore. The boys were invariably (like their counterparts at Round Hill and Flushing) the scions of well-to-do families; Muhlenberg mentioned this situation with regret in a revealing letter to Kerfoot dated 28 January 1851: "So I hear you have been packing off lots of boys. That's right; there is no other way. A church school is not a garden to raise weeds in; but alas! as long as church schools can receive only the children of the rich, they will be raising crops of weeds. You can only do your best by rooting out the most noxious."[16] Despite occasional problems the College prospered and enjoyed a good reputation. Bishop Whittingham, who kept in close touch with Kerfoot throughout the life of the school, told him in a letter of 27 August 1855 that he had recently heard a

---

[14] Brand, 1:288-303; Thomas J. C. Williams, *A History of Washington County, Maryland* (n.p., 1906), 197, 386; David Churchman Trimble, *History of St. John's Church, Hagerstown, Maryland* (Hagerstown, MD, 1981), 34; Harrison, 1:45; McLachlan, "Civil War Diary," 246-47; Edith Rossiter Bevan, "Fountain Rock, The Ringgold Home in Washington County," *MHM* 47 (March 1952): 19-28.

[15] McLachlan, *American Boarding Schools*, 133.

[16] Muhlenberg to Kerfoot, 28 January 1851, in Harrison, 1:136.

report of a conversation in which Jared Sparks (who had completed his term as president of Harvard University not long before) had stated: "By and by, there is one institution in the South which has sent some remarkable exceptions [to the general run of negligent and rowdy students]. It is, I believe, in Maryland, and called the College of St. James. Four or five young men have come from it to Cambridge, and have been without exception among the best prepared and the best mannered men we have."[17]

Kerfoot's institution comprised four "collegiate classes" and, in its grammar school, three "preparatory classes." The degree of Bachelor of Arts was conferred upon those who completed the collegiate studies and satisfactorily passed the requisite examinations. Each class period lasted two hours, the first of which was devoted to preparation and the second to recitation.[18] Accounts of the practice of recitation at

---

[17] As quoted in Whittingham to Kerfoot, 27 August 1855, in Brand, 1:302. Of course, at this period in its history, Harvard itself was not nearly as impressive as it would later become. Henry Adams, Class of 1858, said "No one took Harvard College seriously.... It taught little, and that little ill, but it left the mind open, free from bias, ignorant of facts, but docile." *The Education of Henry Adams: An Autobiography* (Boston, 1918), 54, 55.

[18] *Register of the College of St. James ... for ... 1850-51*, 9-14, 24, 26; John Barrett Kerfoot, *Academical Degrees and Titles: An Address at the Eighth Annual Commencement of the College of St. James ...* (New York, 1854), 19-20. The College catalog indicates that Wilkins during his last two years at St. James's should have studied the following subjects: Sophomore year: Greek (Plato, Xenophon, Acts of the Apostles), Latin (Cicero, Virgil, Horace), mathematics (algebra, trigonometry), chemistry, history (modern period), English (rhetoric, English literature), and sacred studies (Bible, church history). Junior year: Greek (Sophocles, Demosthenes de Corona, Epistle to

nineteenth-century American schools might lead one to suppose that during this classroom exercise the teacher did not interpret or discuss the reading with his young scholars but merely listened and appraised as they read, spelled, summed, or regurgitated memorized material aloud.[19] This situation probably did obtain at many schools but at the College of St. James the process seems to have been more active and dialectical than that. There, according to Joseph H. Coit, who had studied and then taught at St. James's, the students were supposed to prepare their lessons on a given text--e.g., Paley's *Evidences* or Butler's *Analogy*--in such a way that they knew not only the factual content of the chapter assigned but also the author's method of argumentation. Then, in class, they would be asked to discuss the reading, to analyze it and raise objections to it. Next, Kerfoot "would criticize our answers, show where they failed to represent Butler's argument, point out their weakness or double-edgedness, and thus train us, by methods not unlike those of Socrates, to careful habits of thinking and observation, and to a certain just moderation of

---

the Romans), Latin (Tacitus, Horace, Cicero), mathematics (analytical geometry), natural philosophy (mechanics, hydrostatics, pneumatics, heat, acoustics, optics), English (logic, rhetoric, English literature), and sacred studies (Bible, catechism, Thirty-nine Articles, evidences of Christianity). *Register of the College of St. James, 1860* (Baltimore, 1860), 18-20.

[19] See, for example, Jean Baker, *Affairs of Party: The Political Culture of Northern Democrats in the Mid-Nineteenth Century* (Ithaca, NY, 1983), 94, 99.

Reprinted from Harrison, *Life of Kerfoot*, vol. 1, frontispiece.

John Barrett Kerfoot

expression."[20] Students prepared twenty-two recitations each week.[21]

Life at the College of St. James proceeded smoothly until the coming of the Civil War. Then the enrollment declined sharply and no little anxiety began to be felt regarding the school's future. The refusal of Maryland to join the Confederacy and concern over their children's safety led many parents to withdraw their sons from the College. Kerfoot wrote Whittingham on 27 April 1861 that "Most of them [the students] are now secessionists. They know that we are Union men. Yet obedience and harmony, and in most of the classes marked industry, prevail." He feared, though, that this calm would not last: "Our College is in great peril. Border war, apparently inevitable now, must shut it up--and then how long?"[22] At the graduation ceremony on the tenth of July, the rector bravely remarked that St. James's had never enjoyed greater public confidence and indeed had proved over recent months that it could be true to its own principles (including Unionism) and practice Christian toleration at the same time.[23] Late in August of 1861 he placed an advertisement in a

---

[20] Coit, 338. See also the description in Harrison, 22.

[21] *Register of the College of St. James ... for ... 1850-51*, 24; *Register of the College of St. James, 1858* (Baltimore, 1858), 20.

[22] Kerfoot to Whittingham, 27 April 1861, in Harrison, 1:209-10.

[23] *Baltimore American and Commercial Advertiser*, 17 July 1861.

Hagerstown newspaper announcing that the next session would open on Wednesday, the 25th of September; an article in the same paper directed readers' attention to the notice and expressed faith in the perdurability of the College.[24] But in the fall only sixteen students showed up, and though that number rose over succeeding months enrollment after July 1862 never again climbed above fifty.[25]

In normal times St. James's location in the rolling hills and farm country of Washington County was quite tranquil, all that a follower of Emanuel von Fellenberg could ask for in the way of isolation and serenity. But after the spring of 1861 this area underwent a dramatic transformation, finding itself as it did on the main thoroughfare of two opposing armies. Suddenly the College's position became a real detriment to its survival. Soldiers of both sides crossed and recrossed the school grounds, often camping on College property. The battle of Antietam was fought only seven miles away at Sharpsburg, causing the opening of the 1862-1863 session to be delayed over a month. After this engagement, the bloodiest of the war, the rector of St. James's helped to bury the dead, and joined members of his staff on visits to the sick and wounded in nearby hospitals, bringing the soldiers Bibles, biscuits, and chewing tobacco. Five days after the battle of Gettysburg the

---

[24] *Hagerstown Herald of Freedom and Torch Light*, 28 August 1861.

[25] Richard R. Duncan, "The College of St. James: A Casualty of War," *HMPEC* 39 (September 1970): 272.

retreating Confederate army looted the campus, carrying away clothing, foodstuffs, and valuables. Since the burning in 1857 of Kemp Hall (the College's main building, built in 1851), Kerfoot and backers of the College of St. James had made progress toward securing funds for a new, more generally accessible campus twenty miles outside of Baltimore. Now, just when a new site was desperately needed, those plans--and the buildings that had already been started--had to be abandoned. Too many of the College's old friends had become supporters of the Confederacy. The beginning of the end came in July 1864 with the raid into Maryland of General Jubal Early. On 7 August Kerfoot and his assistant, Joseph Coit, were arrested by Confederate officers in retaliation for the seizure by Union troops of the Reverend Hunter Boyd, a Presbyterian minister from Winchester, Virginia. The next day the two men were paroled on condition that they secure Boyd's release, which, after prolonged struggles with the wartime bureaucracy, they did. The College never reopened after the summer of 1864. The same month Kerfoot was arrested by Early's men he received word of his selection by Trinity College in Hartford to become its president. This offer, coupled with concerns about his wife's health and the apparent hopelessness of the College's financial situation, inclined him, with profound regret, to surrender the fight to save St. James's. His arrest and the numerous difficulties the College faced he took as indications of God's will that the enterprise be given up.[26] Bishop Whittingham was deeply affected by the failure of his beloved project. In his address to the diocesan convention in 1865 he said: "What your bishop lost in all this process, brethren, I shall not attempt to tell. For him it makes a large part of the work of a quarter of a century a blank. No future on earth holds out promise of any compensation. There can be no replacement for him of the bonds of almost life-long growth that have been broken."[27]

If there was cause for sorrow over the school's collapse there was also reason for satisfaction in its achievements and for appreciation of the impressive legacy it left to other institutions. In truth, the embers of St. James's were never allowed to go out completely; they were simply moved to other locations, there to blaze up again to help light the way for new founders, rectors, and masters.

---

[26] Heckscher, 42-43; Harrison, 1:180, 187, 189, 235-37, 250, 261, 270; Coit, 356, 361, 362, 368-69; Hall Harrison, "The College of St. James," in *History of Education in Maryland*, ed. Bernard C. Steiner (Washington, 1894), 258-60; Scharf, 2:1239, 1241; *Register of the College of St. James, 1860*, 34; John B. Kerfoot, *An Address Delivered at the Commencement of the College of St. James ... in 1862* (Baltimore, 1862); Richard R. Duncan, "The Impact of the Civil War on Education in Maryland," *MHM* 61 (March 1966): 37-39; McLachlan, "Civil War Diary," 245-60; Duncan, "The College of St. James: A Casualty of War," 265-86. Kerfoot served as president of Trinity College from 1864 to early 1866, when he became first bishop of Pittsburgh. See Harrison, *Life of Kerfoot*; *National Cyclopedia of American Biography* 3:497; *Appleton's Cyclopedia of American Biography*, s.v. "Kerfoot, John Barrett."

[27] Whittingham, as quoted in Brand, 1:293.

The fire was first passed even before the College of St. James closed. In 1855 Dr. George Cheyne Shattuck Jr. founded near Concord, New Hampshire, St. Paul's School, which was to be the most influential model for the dozens of boarding schools established in the decades following the Civil War.[28] Shattuck, an alumnus of Round Hill, lived in Maryland in the 1840s and early '50s and came to know the College of St. James well. His wife, née Anne Henrietta Brune, was a member of a prominent Baltimore family and a devout Episcopalian; she had a younger brother who was a student at St. James's. Dr. Shattuck visited the College frequently and lectured there on anatomy and physiology. He became friends with Bishop Whittingham and John B. Kerfoot; the latter conducted the service in the College chapel in which Shattuck, having decided to leave the Congregationalism of his youth, was received into the Episcopal Church. (It was Shattuck, by the way, who was responsible in 1864 for seeing that Kerfoot was offered the presidency of Trinity College.)[29]

Familiar with the accomplishments of Muhlenberg in New York, well acquainted with the masters and program at the College of St. James, and unwilling to send his own children to an academy, Shattuck decided to start at his

---

[28] McLachlan, *American Boarding Schools*, 136; Skardon, 91.

[29] McLachlan, *American Boarding Schools*, 139, 325 n. 7; Heckscher, 8; *Register of the College of St. James ... for ... 1850-51*, 4; *Register of the College of St. James ... for the Tenth Session, 1851-52* (Baltimore, 1852), 16.

summer residence his own school; one that would be, like Muhlenberg's and Kerfoot's, a sort of Episcopalian Round Hill.[30] The man chosen to be its first rector was Henry Augustus Coit (1830-1895), who had attended St. Paul's College and taught Latin and Greek in the early 1850s at the College of St. James. The schools of Muhlenberg and Kerfoot exerted a powerful influence on Shattuck and Coit's new enterprise; eight masters from St. James's eventually joined the faculty of St. Paul's. Joseph Howland Coit Jr., Henry's younger brother, and Hall Harrison (1837-1900) both journeyed to Concord in 1865 after the closing of the Maryland school. The latter, a graduate of the College of St. James, had taught ancient languages there; at St. Paul's School he was an instructor of Greek and English. Held in high esteem by both students and faculty, he left St. Paul's in 1879 to return to Maryland (and his native town) as rector of St. John's Church, Ellicott City. Joseph Coit (1831-1906) had been a key figure at his alma mater under Kerfoot, and now at St. Paul's assisted his brother as vice rector. He became rector in 1895 after Henry's death.[31]

---

[30] McLachlan, *American Boarding Schools*, 142, 143, 168; Heckscher, 1-3. Students at the academies lived with local families; their lives were not as closely supervised and regulated as their counterparts' were at the boarding schools. Boys at academies were required to attend classes and chapel services but were otherwise beyond the direct control of their institutions.

[31] On Henry A. Coit see Heckscher, 11-17 and passim; *Appleton's Cyclopedia*, s.v., "Coit, Henry Augustus"; *Dictionary of American Biography*, s.v. "Coit, Henry Augustus"; McLachlan, *American Boarding Schools*, 148, 168. On Hall Harrison see Heckscher, 42, 45; J. H. Coit, "Subsequent History," *Memorials of St. Paul's School* (New York, 1891), 52n; *Appleton's*

St. Mark's School in Southborough, Massachusetts, established in 1865, was closely related to St. Paul's, Concord, and to the College of St. James. Its founder, manufacturer Joseph Burnett (1820-1894), had been heavily influenced in his decision to begin the school by Henry Coit; and the first headmaster was John Barrett Kerfoot's nephew, the Reverend John Kerfoot Lewis, who had been a student and then a tutor at St. James's. The example of St. Mark's inspired Endicott Peabody to start a school of his own at Groton. In this quite direct manner was the patrimony--the Fellenbergian example of Cogswell and Bancroft as transformed by Muhlenberg-- passed down the line from one institution to another. The process did resemble what one observer has called "an apostolic succession in the founding of the schools." It might have mitigated Bishop Whittingham's sorrow to know that what he had helped to bring about was being reproduced in a responsible and orderly fashion by other men elsewhere, and that, indeed, rectors of boarding schools could now, fifty years after Round Hill had first opened its doors, use the term "family school" with complete confidence that their listeners would know exactly what they meant.[32]

Cyclopedia, s.v. "Harrison, Hall." On Joseph H. Coit Jr. see Heckscher, 42, 46, and passim; McLachlan, *American Boarding Schools*, 135; *National Cyclopedia of American Biography* 12:466; Prescott Evarts, "Joseph Howland Coit, Rector," *Horae Scholasticae*, 3 April 1906, 184-90.

[32] McLachlan, *American Boarding Schools*, 179-81, 255.

Maryland on the Eve of the Civil War

The convulsion occasioned by secession and civil war that led to the extinction of Bishop Whittingham's diocesan school had been dreaded by most Marylanders as the onset of the tragic conflict approached in 1860-1861. By and large a moderate and conservative people, they were loath to embrace either rebellion against the Union or Federal coercion to hold it together.[33] They hoped somehow to avoid the dislocations and depredations that, once war began, were sure to be visited upon a border state adjoining the capital of the United States. As Barbara Jeanne Fields has written in her recent book on Maryland, the war period as often as not found citizens of the border states "a carping and querulous body of obstructionists, forced willy-nilly to adhere to the Union and forever thereafter resentful that life could not go on quietly as before."[34] Three days after the fall of Fort Sumter, Allen Bowie Davis wrote his son Wilkins at the College of St. James, expressing views that were shared by others in the state: "We here in Maryland I fear are to be the innocent victims of the ... agitation between the North and the South. We have not provoked the contest

---

[33] Donald Marquand Dozer, *Portrait of the Free State: A History of Maryland* (Cambridge, MD, 1976), 438-39; William C. Wright, *The Secession Movement in the Middle Atlantic States* (Cranbury, NJ, 1973), 54, 65.

[34] Barbara Jeanne Fields, *Slavery and Freedom on the Middle Ground: Maryland during the Nineteenth Century* (New Haven, 1985), 91.

and cannot rightfully be made parties to it, but I fear we cannot escape its consequences."[35]

For a period in late 1860 and early 1861 numerous Marylanders--including John Pendleton Kennedy, Benjamin Chew Howard, and Governor Thomas Hicks, as well as Bishop Whittingham and John B. Kerfoot--hoped that Maryland and the other border states might help prevent disunion by forming a "middle confederacy." This regional alliance, they thought, could function as a restraining wall between North and South, giving both sides time to adjust their differences. Representatives of the border states could aid the peace effort by serving as mediators.[36] The last major attempt to find some basis for voluntary reconstruction was the Peace Convention held in Washington in February 1861. There, members of the Maryland delegation, with one exception, acted as brokers betwen the demands of the northern and southern delegations, looking for a means of conciliation that would avert bloodshed. Their work proved to be in vain, however, as the peace conference failed to come up with any fresh proposals to resolve the crisis, after three weeks producing nothing better

---

[35] ABD to WWD, 16 April 1861, ABD Letters. Jean Baker comments that "geographical position made Marylanders fear, quite correctly, that their homes and farms might become a military proving ground." *The Politics of Continuity: Maryland Political Parties from 1858 to 1870* (Baltimore, 1973), 51.

[36] Wright, 30, 46, 49; Harrison, *Life of Kerfoot* 1:194; Baker, *Politics of Continuity*, 50-51.

than a plan that would have allowed the same extension of slavery into the territories as the Crittenden Compromise. Hopes for a counterforce that would prevent war collapsed with the failure of this conference.[37]

The Maryland body politic manifested hesitancy and indecisiveness in the sectional crisis because the state was not exclusively northern or southern but both, tied to the economies and cultures of both sections. Baltimore's textile mills used southern cotton, but its flour mills ground the grain of the Old Northwest. Maryland's political economy was in a period of transition from a premodern structure based on slavery to a capitalist system that employed free labor; hence the state was a social and economic hybrid, now being pulled in opposite directions by the force of circumstances. Maryland politicians took an intermediate stance between the opposed groups because they did not want to choose between them. Spokesmen for each of the contending parties presented reasons why their proposed course of action was the right one.

---

[37] William B. Hesseltine, *Lincoln and the War Governors* (New York, 1948), 154; Carl N. Everstine, *The General Assembly of Maryland 1850-1920* (Charlottesville, VA, 1984), 93; George L. P. Radcliffe, *Governor Thomas H. Hicks of Maryland and the Civil War* (Baltimore, 1901), 37-39; William J. Evitts, *A Matter of Allegiances: Maryland from 1850 to 1861* (Baltimore, 1974), 165 n. 82; Wright, 19; Charles Lewis Wagandt, *The Mighty Revolution: Negro Emancipation in Maryland, 1862-1864* (Baltimore, 1964), 30; Dozer, 443-44; James M. McPherson, *Ordeal by Fire: The Civil War and Reconstruction* (New York, 1982), 138; Bruce Catton, *The Coming Fury*, vol. 1 of *The Centennial History of the Civil War* (Garden City, NY, 1961), 237-38; Baker, *Politics of Continuity*, 52.

Those who supported secession argued that Maryland, southern in its customs and institutions, would benefit economically as a Confederate state: elimination of the tariff on manufactured articles imported from Europe would make those goods cheaper; the state's extensive trade with the South would continue; Virginia would not close off access to the Chesapeake Bay and ruin the state's foreign commerce; and Baltimore, as the South's most important industrial center, could become the New York of the Confederacy. Their opponents pointed out that, if Maryland seceded, it would be cut off from the rest of the South by the Potomac River and open to attack from Pennsylvania and New Jersey; it would lose thousands of dollars worth of slaves who would escape to the North, and there would be no Fugitive Slave Law providing for their return; the Union, with an effective navy, could close the Chesapeake, or keep it open; the Baltimore and Ohio Railroad, which brought raw products from western states for Maryland's mills and manufacturing plants, would be destroyed; and the elimination of the tariff would result in unwanted foreign competiton for Maryland manufacturers and higher taxes throughout the South. In short, the state outside the Union would be more vulnerable in every way.[38]

---

[38] Harold R. Manakee, *Maryland in the Civil War* (Baltimore, 1961), 22; Fields, 6, 22; Evitts, 155; Wright, 22-23; Carl M. Frasure, "Union Sentiment in Maryland, 1859-1861," *MHM* 24 (September 1929): 210-24; Charles Branch Clark, *Politics in Maryland during the Civil War* (Chestertown, MD, 1952), 18-23; Dozer, 439; Sean Wilentz, review of *Slavery and Freedom on the Middle Ground*, by Barbara Jeanne Fields, *American Historical Review* 91 (April 1986): 464-65; Richard R. Duncan, "The Era of the Civil War," in *Maryland:*

Eventually, of course, pro-Union sentiment, prodded by Federal force, prevailed, but not until after elements within the state that were sympathetic with the South had had their day.

Central and western Maryland, where slaves amounted to only about 5% of the total popluation, tended to identify with the North. The most powerful southern sympathies could generally be found in southern Maryland (44% slave) and, to a lesser extent, on the Eastern Shore (20% slave). Feeling was strongest for the South in the tobacco counties of Calvert, Charles, Prince George's, Anne Arundel, and St. Mary's.[39] But, in truth, all over the state could be found citizens who were actively pro-South. In Baltimore on 19 April 1861, agitated residents--it is hard to know how many were acting on political principle and how many were straight-out thugs--attacked the Sixth Massachusetts Regiment as it was moving through the city on its way to the Washington train depot. The crowd hurled cobblestones and fired bullets, and the harried troops fired back. Four soldiers and twelve citizens were killed in the riot and a great many injured. That night, at the home

---

A History, 1632 to 1974, ed. Richard Walsh and William Lloyd Fox (Baltimore, 1974), 333-34.

[39] Everstine, 77, 92, 147; Wright, 54, 21; Fields, 6, 15, 20-21, 93; Dozer, 436; Manakee, 20-21. Fields indicates the dilemma faced by the "... slave portion of Maryland [which] could afford neither separation from the northern counties, where the state's vitality largely resided, nor separation from the slave South, which offered support to the institutional basis of its society" (p. 22). For an interesting description of the situation in Washington County on the eve of the war, see Williams, 304-308.

of Mayor George W. Brown, desperate action was agreed upon to prevent the movement of any more troops through the state: an order was given, apparently with the approval of Governor Hicks, to destroy the railroad bridges on all the major approaches to Baltimore. Subsequent negotiations between Maryland authorities and the Federal government produced a pledge from the latter that no more troops would be sent through Baltimore; they would instead be taken by steamer from Perryville (a Unionist town at the north end of the Bay) to Annapolis and then to Washington.[40] The secession forces, in the wake of the 19 April riot, were temporarily masters of public sentiment; but, because of the Lincoln administration's caution, passions cooled and Unionism reasserted itself.[41]

After the dramatic events of April 1861, Maryland moved closer to accepting its place within the Union and the requirements this position would entail. In mass meetings throughout the state, in Governor Hicks's improved relations with the government of the United States, in the conduct of the legislature, and in the success of military operations in Maryland, progress could be seen toward the solidification of support for the Union. Over time Marylanders gave up the idea that they could assume a stance of "armed neutrality," according to which they would defend their own ground but

---

[40] Everstine, 94, 95, 97; Hesseltine, 155; Radcliffe, 50-57, 61; Manakee, 38, 42; White, 155; Fields, 93, 94; Evitts, 176-84.

[41] Evitts, 183.

refuse to participate in the conflict elsewhere. Indeed, while many were attempting to remain above the fray, the U.S. government was strengthening its hold on the state. Before the end of April, Fort McHenry was reinforced heavily and teams of men were put to work rebuilding the railway bridges. On 5 May Union General Benjamin F. Butler seized control of Relay House, an important railroad junction southwest of Baltimore where the line to Washington and the B. & O.'s main line to the West came together. A week later he entered Baltimore under cover of a violent evening thunderstorm with a thousand men; residents of the city awoke in the morning to find well-protected batteries aimed at Monument Square. The state legislature, meeting in Frederick from late April to the middle of May, declined for the moment to try to take Maryland out of the Union. By the time the General Assembly reconvened in June, Governor Hicks and the Federal authorities dominated the state and the legislators could take no disloyal action. Now the troops Lincoln had asked for were recruited and no qualification was made regarding their place of service. In a special election held on 13 June, pro-Union candidates carried sixteen of the state's twenty-one counties. In September, U.S. officials, in an unnecessary move of questionable legality, arrested a large number of state legislators, as well as Mayor Brown and Congressman-elect Henry May of Baltimore, holding them at various Federal forts for periods of time ranging from several months to over two years. None ever had formal charges placed against him.[42] For the duration of the war the Lincoln administration suppressed Confederate sympathies in Maryland, bringing government authority to bear against newspapers, private citizens, and even clergymen.[43]

In the November 1861 elections, Augustus W. Bradford, the Union party candidate, defeated States' Rightist Benjamin C. Howard, and pro-Union men gained control of the state legislature. Some have said their election was brought about by Federal bayonets, but recent scholarship has disputed the charge of widespread military initmidation and coercion of voters.[44] The legislature met in a special session in December and again in a regular session that ran from January to March. Members took strong stands in favor of the Union, though they made it clear at the same time that they wished to bolster the institution of slavery. They pressed for enforcement of the

---

[42] Evitts, 185-91; Hesseltine, 213-14; Radcliffe, 58; Manakee, 52; Baker, *Politics of Continuity*, 55-58; Wright, 71-73; Fields, 98-100; Everstine, 114-15, 117-18; Catton, 354-56; Allan Nevins, *The War for the Union: The Improvised War, 1861-1862*, vol. 5 of *The Ordeal of the Union* (New York, 1959), 87; Clark, 2, 39-40, 61, 63. As Clark points out, Lincoln regarded "armed neutrality" as disloyalty and a serious threat to the Union. Supplies could be passed more freely to rebels under the guise of neutrality than they could by an open enemy. Armed neutrality would have given the rebels disunion without a struggle. States had an obligation, Lincoln felt, to maintain the Union; neutrality was injurious to that aim. Clark, 39-40.

[43] Fields, 98-100.

[44] See Baker, *Politics of Continuity*, 71-74.

Fugitive Slave Law and for means to secure reimbursement of slaveowners for the loss of slaves caused by wartime conditions. Governor Bradford spoke in his inaugural address of the twin miseries of secession and abolitionism. In office he upheld the Federal government's authority though he disagreed with its methods in his state. The November 1861 election and its aftermath demonstrated that Maryland was now definitely lost to the secessionists.[45] Indeed, although Maryland's secession movement had been quite vigorous, Unionism had probably always been stronger in the state than disloyalty. As historian Wiliam J. Evitts has commented, "Barring the April 19 riot, the record of Maryland shows more fear of the consequences of war that it shows any entrenched treason. The entire 'armed neutrality' notion was the product not of disloyalty but of dismay. By 1861 Maryland had evolved into a pattern of life so different from that of the Southern states that secession was never more than a distant possibility."[46]

---

[45] Everstine, 147-53, 169; Hesseltine, 237; Radcliffe, 116, 119-20; Manakee, 56, 60; White, 159-63; Clark, 87-94; Baker, *Politics of Continuity*, 71-74.

[46] Evitts, 190. Of the five Middle Atlantic states, Maryland had the strongest secession movement. Wright, 21.

The Episcopal Church in Maryland

The strife that afflicted the state of Maryland during the Civil War rent the diocese as well.[47] At the national level the Episcopal Church handled the problems caused by secession and military conflict gracefully.[48] The ecclesiastical situation in Maryland required a similar application of tact and prudence to prevent dissension and lasting animosities. What it received was the leadership of William Rollinson Whittingham, a learned, patriotic, willful man, of whom Thomas March Clark, bishop of Rhode Island, wrote: "He liked to have his own way when he felt certain that he was right, and that was a conviction which did not often fail him."[49] Clearly Whittingham believed he was right about the controversies now facing Marylanders. While he thought that slaveholding was lawful and abolition a crime, he viewed slavery itself as a great evil and opposed allowing it to spread beyond its present limits. He understood the rebellion of the South to be a grave breach of divine law and approved of the use of Federal troops to force the seceded states back into the

---

[47] The Maryland diocese in 1860 consisted of 130 churches and approximately 11,000 parishioners.

[48] For an account of the wartime Episcopal Church in both the North and the South see S. D. McConnell, *History of the American Episcopal Church: From the Planting of the Colonies to the End of the Civil War* (New York, 1890), 360-73.

[49] Thomas M. Clark, *Reminiscences* (New York, 1895), 131-32.

Union and to suppress disloyal sentiment in the border states. He was adamant in his demand that clergy of the diocese not omit the prayer for the president of the United States in their conduct of the services, regarding its exclusion as a mutilation of the liturgy and a violation of the ordination vows. When Lincoln proclaimed days of national fasting or thanksgiving, Whittingham issued pastoral letters in which he set forth the prayers to be used on those occasions. The Reverend Charles C. Grafton, who eventually became bishop of Fond du Lac, served in the early 1860s as an assistant to the Reverend William E. Wyatt at Old St. Paul's in Baltimore. His description of his own experience indicates the difficulties faced by clergy throughout the diocese during "... a most trying political time. I had felt it my duty ... to read the pastorals which Bishop Whittingham, who was a most decided Unionist, put forth. They were couched in very trenchant language, and with quotations from the homilies on the sin and wickedness of rebellion. During the illness of the rector, when I was forced to read them, I can well remember the way the pew doors were slammed and the people left during their delivery." He added: "A number of Confederate church people loved me for my ministrations, but when a vacancy occurred in the rectorship the people naturally chose a southerner to succeed Dr. Wyatt."[50]

---

[50] Charles C. Grafton, *A Journey Godward* (Milwaukee, 1910), 35; Brand, 2:1, 5-6, 8, 15, 18-19, 25-27; Nelson Waite Rightmyer, "The Church in a Border State--Maryland," *HMPEC* 17 (December 1948): 411-12, 414-15; Richard R. Duncan, "Bishop Whittingham, the Maryland Diocese, and the Civil War," *MHM* 61 (December 1966): 329-35. At the College of St. James

Not all priests were as obedient as Grafton. When some refused to read the offending prayers or to hold services on specially appointed days, their diocesan presented them to the Standing Committee--which then refused to take any action against them.[51] When Whittingham expressed his support for a bill that had been introduced in the Maryland House of Delegates that would have required ordained ministers to sign an oath of loyalty to the Federal government, clergy in his diocese openly expressed their resentment and disapproval of what they took to be an Erastian usurpation of their rights.[52]

Whittingham's desire to see men as fervently Unionist as he elected to various positions in the diocese was frustrated by the course of events. When the diocesan convention met in May of 1862, a new slate was put forward in opposition to the old Standing Committee--and as a deliberate move to block the bishop's power to have recusant clergy tried for disobedience. With the exception of Dr. William E. Wyatt, who had served for years as the committee's president, a new group--all southern sympathizers--were chosen to fill the seats.

---

eighteen or twenty boys walked out in protest when the rector, at Whittingham's behest, read prayers in chapel that they found offensive. Harrison, 1:227.

[51] Brand, 2:23-24; Rightmyer, 415-16; Duncan, "Bishop Whittingham," 334-35.

[52] Brand, 2:28-29; Rightmyer, 416-17; Duncan, "Bishop Whittingham," 336-38.

In addition, Hugh Davey Evans, a well-known layman (and occasional lecturer on civil and ecclesiastical law at the College of St. James), was defeated in his bid for reelection as deputy to the General Convention because of his Unionist views.[53] In 1863 problems arising over the composition of its board of trustees threatened to close down the College of St. James. Whittingham was unwilling to accede to Kerfoot's request that he appoint three men who were known to be southern sympathizers to the school's board. The rector of St. James's told the bishop his refusal would bring about the resignation of the present board and the departure of two-thirds of the student body. Whittingham finally retreated and accepted Kerfoot's proposal that trustees be selected on the basis of residence near the College rather than on the basis of political beliefs.[54]

Here and there in the diocese individual parishes were riven by discord caused by the sectional conflict. Dr. Arthur Cleveland Coxe, rector of Grace Church in Baltimore, narrowly missed being evicted by the pro-South group in his church.[55] In Frederick the rector of All Saints Parish, the Reverend Charles Seymour, met similar opposition in 1862 and felt it better to resign than to stay. A resident of the city, Jacob

---

[53] Brand, 2:29-31; Edward N. Todd, "The 'Recollections' of Hugh Davey Evans," *HMPEC* 34 (December 1965): 331; Rightmyer, 417.

[54] Harrison, *Life of Kerfoot* 1:254-58; Duncan, "Bishop Whittingham," 340-41.

[55] Duncan, "Bishop Whittingham," 338-40.

Engelbrecht, noted in his diary that the priest was "a thorough Union man and Some of his Parishoners are Rebels Siding with the Infamous Rebellion."[56]

The Davis Family

Before turning to the letters, some information ought to be given about the family of W. Wilkins Davis. He was the last male descendant of a long and distinguished line of Davises stretching back to Thomas Davis (the elder), who came to America from Wales and settled in Maryland around 1690. Thomas's grandson, Ephraim Davis (1736-1769), built "Greenwood," the family home in Montgomery County, on land purchased by his father, Thomas Davis Jr. (1704-1749). Ephriam's son, Thomas Davis III (1768-1833), commanded a company that went to Pennsylvania in 1794 to quell the Whiskey Rebellion. He was also a member of the House of Delegates, a vestryman at his parish church (St. Bartholomew's), president of the board of trustees of Brookeville Academy (a nearby private school), and an associate judge of the county court. In 1802 he married Elizabeth Bowie, daughter of Allen Bowie Jr. Their son was Allen Bowie Davis (1809-1889), who, at the age of twenty-four,

---

[56] *The Diary of Jacob Englebrecht* (Frederick, MD, 1976), 3:157 (entry for 22 May 1862).

Reprinted from Scharf, *History of Western Maryland,* vol. 1, facing p. 771.

Greenwood

Greenwood Today

took over the operation of the estate at Greenwood.[57] This property was located two miles north of Brookeville, a village ten miles northeast of Rockville, eighteen miles north of the District of Columbia, and forty-two miles west of Baltimore. Bowie Davis (as he was known) was a prosperous planter; by 1850 he had twenty-seven slaves to assist him in growing tobacco and cereal crops, in caring for the livestock (cattle, sheep, hogs), in tending his extensive apple orchards, and in running a grist mill, a cider mill and press, and a sawmill. By 1860 he had increased the size of the home farm to 1,066 acres and owned two other farms not far away as well as a winter residence in Baltimore and other properties in that city and in Brookeville.[58]

Allen Bowie Davis married Rebecca Comfort Dorsey, daughter of Judge Thomas Beale Dorsey of Howard County, in

---

[57] J. Montgomery Seaver, *Davis Family Records* (Philadelphia, n.d.), 20 (in Genealogy file, Montgomery County Historical Society, Rockville); "Allen Bowie Davis," The Montgomery County Courier, 20 October 1976; Biographical Cyclopedia of Representative Men of Maryland and the District of Columbia (Baltimore, 1879), 346; Roger Brooke Farquhar, Historic Montgomery County, Maryland, Old Homes and History (Silver Spring, MD, 1952), 177-81; Walter Worthington Bowie, The Bowies and Their Kindred (Washington, 1899), 92-93.

[58] T. H. S. Boyd, *The History of Montogomery County, Maryland, from ... 1650 to 1879* (1879; reprint, Baltimore, 1972), 122; George W. Howard, *The Monumental City* (Baltimore, 1873), 649; *Maryland Slave Schedule 1850* (microfilm, MHS); *Maryland Census 1850* (microfilm, MHS); Roger Brooke Farquhar, "Greenwood," Historic Houses file, Montgomery County Historical Society. The address of Greenwood today is 21315 Georgia Avenue (Route 97).

Reprinted, by permission of the Montgomery Mutual Insurance Company, from *Mutual Fire Insurance Company of Montgomery County: The Eightieth Anniversary* (Baltimore, 1928).

Allen Bowie Davis

1830. She died without children in 1836, at the age of twenty-seven. In 1839 Davis married Hester Ann Wilkins (1809-1888), daughter of a prominent Baltimore dry goods merchant, William Wilkins. They had six children: Thomas (11 August 1840-3 February 1849), William Wilkins (27 March 1842-2 March 1866), Rebecca Dorsey (23 December 1843-5 April 1921), Mary Dorsey (9 September 1845-17 January 1939), Esther Wilkins (29 November 1847-23 November 1894), and Allen Bowie (d. 20 September 1850, age nine months).[59] Wilkins's sisters were often away at boarding school when he was at the College of St. James.

While he was active in his church and in community affairs, Allen Bowie Davis's primary concern was always agriculture. Indeed, he was a farmer at an interesting time in the history of Montgomery County. By 1840 the soil there had been depleted through the relentless cultivation of tobacco and corn. Land values fell and the population of the county had started to decline. In 1844, though, a new fertilizer was introduced in the county that revived the tired soil. The use of guano, made from the droppings of sea birds, increased corn and wheat yields markedly. Montgomery County farmers were in the vanguard of Marylanders seeking to develop and apply scientific methods of farming, and Bowie Davis was one of the leading agriculturalists in his county and in the state. He was a

---

[59] Davis Family Cemetery, Greenwood; Bowie, 93-95; Genealogy index, Montgomery County Historical Society; Howard, 646.

Maryland Historical Society, Baltimore

Esther Wilkins Davis

Maryland Historical Society, Baltimore

Mary Dorsey Davis

founder of the Montgomery County Agricultural Society (1846), president of the board of trustees of the Maryland Agricultural College (soon to be taken over as a major component of the new University of Maryland), and president of the Maryland Agricultural Society. He was one of the first in the county to use the Hussey reaper and even published an article about the machine. He assisted other farmers by working successfuly in the late 1840s to have tolls on fertilizers reduced on the Chesapeake and Ohio Canal and on the local railroads. He purchased guano in massive quantities and resold it in smaller, unadulterated lots to other growers at affordable rates. The period 1850 to 1860, thanks in part to the efforts of men like Davis, became a time of unrivaled prosperity for many farmers in Montgomery County.[60]

Allen Bowie Davis, like his father, was a local leader, participating in a variety of endeavors designed to benefit the region. His main projects--after agriculture--were education and transportation. One of his first assignments in the community was presiding over the board of trustees of Brookeville Academy. While in office the trustees successfully

---

[60] Bowie, 93; Scharf, 1:673; Esther B. Stabler, "Triadelphia: Forgotten Maryland Town," *MHM* 43 (June 1948): 116; Vivian Wiser, "Improving Maryland's Agriculture, 1840-1860," *MHM* 64 (Summer 1969): 128; Ray Eldon Hiebert and Richard K. MacMaster, *A Grateful Remembrance: The Story of Montgomery County, Maryland* (Rockville, MD, 1976), 126-27, 129; George M. Anderson, "The Montgomery County Agricultural Society: The Beginning Years, 1846-1850," *MHM* 81 (Winter 1986): 305-307, 312; Farquhar, *Historic Montgomery County*, 37-38; George H. Calcott, *A History of the University of Maryland* (Baltimore, 1966), 137, 140; Howard, 648.

petitioned the legislature to prohibit the sale of intoxicants within one mile of the school. Davis, good Whig that he was, looked back with pride on this early achievement for the rest of his life. One of his last duties was to sit on the county board of public school commissioners. He also sought to enhance general literacy and culture through his work for the Brookeville Circulating Library Association. In transportation, he obtained the charter and stock subscription for the Baltimore and Washington Turnpike Company, supervised construction of the road, and guided the company to financial health before retiring after sixteen years' service. He was a member of the state Board of Public Works and a director of the Cheaspeake and Ohio Canal Company. Davis also served for many years as a vestryman of St. Bartholomew's Parish and as a director of the Mutual Fire Insurance Company. It was fitting, given his long years of service to his community, that he was the person chosen to chair the Montgomery County centennial celebration in September 1876.[61]

Davis and his cousin, Richard Johns Bowie (1807-1881), a prominent lawyer, were for years two of the most influential Whigs in a county that, through the 1840s and into the 1850s, was largely Whig. Politics captured Davis's interest

---

[61] Boyd, 96-97; *Annals of Sandy Spring or Twelve Years History of a Rural Community in Maryland* (Baltimore, 1902), 2:157; Howard, 648; Scharf, 1:782; Roger Brooke Farquhar, *Old Homes and History of Montgomery County, Maryland* (Silver Spring, MD, 1952), 82, 209-10; Jane C. Sween, *Montgomery County: Two Centuries of Change* (Woodland Hills, CA, 1984), 82.

particularly when special challenges arose. Though the image is too exalted for a man of his rather modest stature, he did at times, like Cincinnatus, abandon his plow to fulfill his duty in the public arena. On one of these occasions he represented his county at the convention held in 1850-1851 to reform the state constitution. There he opposed a plan to reduce the number of delegates the county was allotted in the General Assembly from four to two and pushed hard as a member of the committee on education for a state school system. He acquitted himself well, winning admiration for the energy and knowledge he displayed in the course of the debates.[62] The other period of unusually active political involvement on his part began in 1860. Of course by this time the Whig party was defunct. Davis turned first to the Constitutional Union party, whose positions on the great issues of the day were consonant with his own, and supported the John Bell-Edward Everett ticket in the November election. After its failure Davis, though a slaveholder and a man with deep southern sympathies, chose to affiliate himself with the Union party.

As one would expect in an area where in 1860 slaves made up 30% of the population, Montgomery County citizens by and large were kindly disposed toward the South and were

---

[62] Bowie, 94, 149-52; Hiebert and MacMaster, 139, 145, 147-48; Anderson, 308; L. E. Blauch, "Education and the Maryland Constitutional Convention, 1850-1851," *MHM* 25 (June 1930): 188; George M. Anderson, "A Delegate to the 1850-51 Constitutional Convention: James W. Anderson of Montgomery County," *MHM* 76 (Fall 1981): 250; ABD, "To the People of Montgomery County," 26 August 1850, ABD Letters.

closely divided on the secession question. Their principal weekly newspaper, the *Sentinel*, urged them regularly in inflammatory editorials to support withdrawal from the Union. An important meeting was held on 1 January 1861 at the county courthouse in Rockville to determine popular sentiment regarding the sectional controversy. Both Unionists, who were old Whigs for the most part, and secessionists, who were largely Democrats, attended the gathering. Allen Bowie Davis and Richard Johns Bowie were the leaders of the pro-Union group. They were able to win support for motions that expressed sympathy for fellow Southerners and outrage at "unconstitutional assults" upon the institution of slavery but that stopped short of calling for secession. Resolutions were adopted declaring the following: slavery is a right the government is obligated to protect, abolition would be detrimental to Maryland, free states should not be permitted to pass laws hindering the recapture of fugitive slaves (personal liberty laws), and Maryland and other border states should convene to protect their constitutional rights. A motion saying Maryland should withdraw from the Union if the issue of slavery was not settled quickly was tabled.[63] On 10 August Montgomery County Unionists met to select delegates to a party convention that was to take place in Baltimore later that month. Bowie Davis was one of the five delegates chosen at this meeting, which also passed a number of pro-Union

---

[63] Hiebert and MacMaster, 152, 162, 167-68, 179; Sween, 69-70; Farquhar, *Historic Montgomery County*, 28.

resolutions.[64] In November Davis was elected to the House of Delegates, where he represented his county in the sessions held during the winter of 1861-1862.[65]

Allen Bowie Davis's politics in the Civil War period were consistently those of a conservative Unionist. In 1862, when Montgomery County Unionists met in Rockville to deplore the abolition of slavery in the District of Columbia and to call for enforcement of the Fugitive Slave Act, Davis was one of the three men who drafted the resolutions of the meeting. In 1863 Unionists in Maryland split into two factions. The Unconditional Unionists, led by Henry Winter Davis, supported emancipation. They advocated the enlistment of black soldiers and were soon agitating for a state constitutional convention to abolish slavery. Allen Bowie Davis remained loyal to the regular Union party organization and to Brantz Mayer, chairman of the Union State Central Committee.

---

[64] Clark, 64.

[65] Davis's legislative record may be traced in the *Journal of the Proceedings of the House of Delegates of the State of Maryland, at a Special Session, December, 1861* (Annapolis, 1861) and in the *Journal of ... Proceedings ... January Session, 1862* (Annapolis, 1862). There are ambiguities in this record, however, because of his failure to vote either yea or nay on several important bills concerning the war. For example, Davis was in attendance for the morning roll call of House members on 27 February 1862, the day of the vote on the "Maryland Defence Loan." The purpose of this loan was to raise the funds necessary to cover Maryland's portion of the direct tax levied by the U.S. government to pay for suppressing the rebellion. No vote is recorded for Davis on this bill. He clearly was present later in the day, though, because he registered his vote on several noncontroversial bills. *Journal of ... Proceedings ... 1862*, 607, 616-17, 622-24.

Mayer, a prominent Baltimore lawyer, opposed abolition, feeling that Maryland was already overburdened with free blacks. Bowie Davis did not accept emancipation until he was forced to do so.[66]

The Davises were a deeply religious family. They regularly attended services at St. Bartholomew's, their parish church, founded in 1812 and located near the Hawlings River, and at its offspring, St. John's, Mechanicsville (now Olney), founded in 1845. Both churches (St. Bartholomew's moved to Laytonsville in 1909) are now in the Diocese of Washington, which was established in 1895. Although Bowie Davis held the positions in the parish, one gathers from the parents' and children's correspondence that the mother, Hester Ann Wilkins Davis, was really the family's spiritual mainstay. She advised her children on sacred (and many other) matters, read religious texts, and even wrote an occasional article for a denominational magazine. Although she often worshiped with her family in the local Episcopal churches, she herself was a Methodist (like her mother) and frequently travelled to hear local preachers of that denomination (usually in Brookeville or Triadelphia) and to attend camp meetings, which were

---

[66] Clark, 169; Fields, 121-22; Wagandt, 101; ABD to Brantz Mayer, 14 May 1863, Brantz Mayer Papers, MS. 581.1, MHS; Hiebert and MacMaster, 179; Bernard C. Steiner, "Brantz Mayer," *MHM* 5 (March 1910): 1-2, 6, 8. See Baker, *Politics of Continuity*, chapter 4, "'The Odium of Faction': Division within the Unionist Party, 1862-1864."

Maryland Historical Society, Baltimore

Hester Ann Wilkins Davis

organized by the Methodists.[67] Her letters, excerpts from which are quoted below, reveal a woman of intelligence, compassion, and fortitude.

The rector of St. Bartholomew's (and of St. John's after its founding) was the Reverend Orlando Hutton (1851-1891). A native of Annapolis, he was ordained in 1837 and began his tenure at St. Bartholomew's in 1844. He served there until 1868. After the Civil War he started a school for girls--St. Anna's Hall--in Brookeville.[68] Hutton's views on the crisis of 1860-1861 were presented to his congregation in a sermon he delivered on 4 January 1861. A. B. Davis liked what his rector said that day well enough to ask him for a copy of his text and for permission to have it printed--and so the sermon survives to this day. Hutton's southern sympathies come through clearly in this discourse. Indeed, he was himself a slaveowner: he worked his three slaves on a farm he owned near Brookeville.[69] He told his parishioners that this "great national

---

[67] Sween, 53, 60, 63; Boyd, 116-18. Mrs. Davis wrote for the *Christian Advocate*, a Methodist journal. HAD to WWD, 21 February 1859, ABD Letters. In her diary she commented on the preaching of the local Episcopal priest: "Mr. Huttons discourses never interest me. They are too superficial.... Hence the spiritual seed sewn in this parish bears no fruit." HAD diary, 15 May 1859, ABD Papers, Box 3. The Methodists grew rapidly in the nineteenth century to become Montgomery County's largest denomination; their particular *bête noire* was liquor. Hiebert and MacMaster, 70, 196.

[68] Hiebert and MacMaster, 192; Ethan Allen, *Clergy in Maryland of the Protestant Episcopal Church* (Baltimore, 1860), 54-55; Scharf, 1:772.

[69] *Maryland Slave Census Schedule 1850*; Boyd, 122.

crisis" would not have arisen had it not been for northern agitation over the slavery question. "It is no more than truth and justice to say that the spirit of abolitionism has been the chief cause in bringing upon us these troubles." But he evidenced in his remarks his hesitation concerning secession: "submission to governments and submission to civil magistrates are enjoined as positive Christian duties." He hoped that prayer and a renewed reliance on Christian principles might bring the two sections together and "assuage this bitterness of feeling."[70] No doubt many in his congregation and in his county felt the same way and shared the same hopes.

    The letters that W. Wilkins Davis, his parents, and his sisters wrote back and forth to one another served a variety of purposes. As Steven M. Stowe has pointed out in a recent article on planter family letters, this correspondence provided parents and children with a means of maintaining the reality of the family across time and distance. Father and mother could exhort a son or daughter away at school to hold to high ideals, to be virtuous, and to work hard to make a good record; and the letters parents received could be read as indications of the extent to which the boarding school was having the desired effect. More and more attention was being paid in the antebellum years to adolescence as a significant and frequently difficult time in a person's life. Letters served as proof to their

---

[70] O. Hutton, *The True Refuge in National Trouble* (Baltimore, 1861), 7-10.

recipients that the old ties were still there; they were a way to communicate love as well as concepts of duty and honor. Certainly this is true of the letters that follow, which do appear to have constituted, to borrow a phrase from Stowe, "the prized center" of Davis family relations.[71]

---

[71] Steven M. Stowe, "The Rhetoric of Authority: The Making of Social Values in Planter Family Correspondence," *Journal of American History* 73 (March 1987): 916-33.

II
THE LETTERS OF W. WILKINS DAVIS

Wilkins at Mr. Prentiss's School

The first time W. Wilkins Davis went to school away from home he attended not the College of St. James but the small school run by Colonel John Prentiss in Medfield, a community on the edge of the Baltimore County mill town of Hampden-Woodberry.[1] Wilkins was a student there when he was between the ages of twelve and fifteen, from the fall of 1854 to the spring of 1857. An early account of his academic progress is included in a letter to him from his father. A. B. Davis told Willy (as his family called him when he was a boy) that Mr. Prentiss felt he was doing well; the teacher's only complaint had to do with "your old habit of wandering thoughts, and too easy abstraction from your books."[2] But both parents were consistently concerned with more than just their son's intellectual training. In February of his first year at Prentiss's, Wilkins wrote his mother (in a letter no longer in existence) requesting her opinion on his taking dancing lessons.

---

[1] J. Thomas Scharf, *History of Baltimore City and County* (Philadelphia, 1881), 838; D. Randall Beirne, "Hampden-Woodberry: The Mill Village in an Urban Setting," *MHM* 77 (Spring 1982): 6, 10.

[2] ABD to WWD, 18 December 1854, ABD Letters.

Her reply made it clear she did not like the idea: "Dancing merely as a bodily exercise, I consider harmless, but my judgment condemns it, from its invariable accompanyments, lightness, frivolity, night-revellings, balls, the intoxicating draught, superfluous dress, evil associations and intense love of the world, all of which are expressly forbidden."[3] On another occasion she exhorted him to "be more studious. Mr. Prentiss ... says you are getting on <u>reasonably well</u>, but thinks you might be more industrious without any danger of injury to your health or mental organization." She treated of his education by relating it to his larger responsibility within the family: "You are my only son, your sisters only brother and in case of your fathers death their only earthly protection. Thus the hopes of your family center in you. Improve the passing moments as they fly. Habits form the character and become second nature. Form then good habits."[4]

Five letters survive from Wilkins's days at this school. The first is from the fall of his first year away. He told one of his sisters "I will send you some tracts which were given to me last Sunday. I will tell you all about it, as I and some of the other boys were setting on the fence a gentleman came up the road on horseback when he had got nearly past us he turned and rode up to the fence and put his hand into his pocket and pulled out some tracts he gave me tow and the other boy one a

---

[3] HAD to WWD, 7 February 1855, ABD Letters.

[4] HAD to WWD, 18 June [1855, '56, or '57], ABD Letters.

piece his name was Mr Flint and he [said] that he had bin to town to preach." Willy's second letter was written a year and a half later. A childhood friend of his had just died: "I was sitting at the Piano yesterday evening and I said to my selfe poor Bill I expect he is dead by this and if he has I hope he has gone to heaven just came from town and I said I expect Mrs. Prentiss has got a letter for me telling me that Bill is dead and sure enough when I went to supper Mrs Prentiss gave me a letter I could not help crying when I read it I remembered how brother Tommy Bill and myself used play in in the dyneing room...."[5]

In the fall of 1856, his mother wrote him a letter in which she revealed her religious faith and some of her political views: "How grateful you ought to feel for the advantages you enjoy, and how very diligent and assiduous you ought to be to improve them. I am sorry to see you so interested in politics. I do think the Union safe. I think, He who rides upon the storm, and holds the whirlwind in his hand, will control the surging billows of political strife; and the good old ship of State which our ancestors so successfully guided, with the Star Spangled banner floating proudly at her prow will steer clear of all the rocks and quick sand, of demagogueism, and be moored safely in <u>Fillmore Harbur</u>."[6] Willy's father shared his wife's

---

[5] WWD to sister, 10 October 1854, ABD Papers, Box 1; WWD to sister, 24 April 1856, ABD Letters.

[6] HAD to WWD, 2 October 1856, ABD Letters.

enthusiasm for the ex-president, who was running at the head of the Know Nothing ticket although he was actually campaigning as an old Whig, paying little heed to the American party's official nativism. A. B. Davis told his son on 17 October that he himself was "an old consistent Whig" and that he had been giving speeches for Fillmore.[7] (The former president went on to gain 44% of the vote in the South but only 13% in the North. Of course he lost to James Buchanan.)

    Wilkins's third surviving letter dates from 29 January 1857. Mr. Prentiss's son was sick with "the measel's" and Mrs. Prentiss was "very sick with the "Plurisy." There was in fact so much sickness that school had not been held for a week. "My business for the last week has been to set the table and attend to the house keeping the boys call me head waiter." Someone had given Willy a dog, which remained at Greenwood. He told his sisters, to whom this letter was addressed: "You must take great care of the puppy.... I think that I will name him Cerberus who was Pluto's three headed dog who gaurded the infernal regions to prevent the living from entering and the dead from escaping from the place of there confinement he could only be put to sleep by a kind of cake."[8] Several days later Wilkins wrote his sister Mary to tell her Mrs. Prentiss had died. "When I came down this morning Mr Prentiss put his arm around my

---

[7] Daniel Walker Howe, *The Political Culture of the American Whigs* (Chicago, 1979), 249; ABD to WWD, 17 October 1856, ABD Letters.

[8] WWD to sisters, 29 January 1857, ABD Letters.

neck and kissed me and said O! my dear boy how do you feel this morning the last words that Mrs Prentiss said were about you and he burst out crying."[9] His letter five days later gave more news: "Mrs Prentiss was buried in the Masoleum at Green Mount not 20 steps from grand Pa Wilkinses vault. As you dont like Cerberus I think I will name my dog Fillmore but if you do not like that you may call him Juno. Tell Ma that while I was playing yesterday I got the coat that I had for best last Winter torn in half it is so rotten that it was not worth mending so gave it to one of the servants for quilt patches."[10] His father next wrote to say he liked the story of Cerberus that Wilkins had related to his sister and now wanted him to send home each week a sketch of the characters he was reading about in Virgil.[11] Mary wrote on 16 February and reproved her brother for not sending any of his sisters valentines.[12]

The final letter to be referred to from this period provides a good link to Wilkins's letters from the College of St. James, which will be quoted below in full. Allen Bowie Davis told his son on 20 February 1857 that "your letters are becoming more and more interesting, as you improve in style as well as hand writing, which we are very much gratified to

---

[9] WWD to MDD, 3 February 1857, ABD Letters.

[10] WWD to sister, 8 February 1857, ABD Letters.

[11] ABD to WWD, 13 February 1857, ABD Letters.

[12] MDD to WWD, 16 February 1857, ABD Letters.

see, and we wish to have you without excuse for practicing so necessary a part of your education--and so beautiful an accomplishment: upon the arrival of the mail yours is the first letter opened."[13]

Wilkins at the College of St. James

Wilkins began his career at the College of St. James in October of 1857. Because of his age, however, he was required to stay back one year in the Grammar School and so was actually a member of the class of 1862, which comprised twenty-two boys. None of the letters he wrote during his first semester survives. Several from his parents that do remain provide a glimpse of his early progress at the school. His father told him on 20 November 1857 that "... we are all very much gratified not to have heard any word of complaint from you since your residence at St. James." He asked his son "to write me a full account of your progress at St. James, and what they say about its removal to Balto county."[14] His mother wrote him on 28 November to ask about his coming home for Christmas and to stress the importance of good manners and knowledge of the Bible. Apparently she had lately received

---

[13] ABD to WWD, 20 February 1857, ABD Letters.

[14] ABD to WWD, 20 November 1857, ABD Letters ; *Register of the College of St. James, 1858*, 13.

one of the school's monthly grade reports, giving marks in courses (on a scale of one to nine) and the student's disciplinary record. "Your number for sacred studies was 5 this is low, but I know you find it difficult to commit verbatim so many verses consecutively.... I am thankful you are obliged to memorize so frequently the sacred text." She spoke of those who had memorized whole books of the Bible. "Now dont think twenty verses much after this. Now do not ask ... Ma for sympathy, but put your shoulder manfully to the wheel and success must be your reward."[15] On 9 December Allen Bowie Davis expressed strong support for his wife, saying, "I doubt whether any boy in college is blessed with a mother so capable to advise, and so conscientious in instruction, as you have."[16]

In the following letter Wilkins mentions a "Mr. Hutton." This was Richard Graham Hutton (1838-1876), younger brother of the Reverend Orlando Hutton and a tutor in history at the College of St. James as well as a recent (1857) graduate of the institution. Like Muhlenberg, Kerfoot employed young men not long out of college to teach and live among the boys, acting as elder brothers within the school family. These men often went into the ministry. Richard Hutton went on to become a priest after studying at General Theological

---

[15] *Register of the College of St. James, 1858*, 21; HAD to WWD, 28 [November] 1857, ABD Letters.

[16] ABD to WWD, 9 December 1857, ABD Letters.

Seminary.[17] The hymn Wilkins quotes is a somewhat distorted version of William A. Muhlenberg's "Carol, brothers, carol."

W. Wilkins Davis to Hester Ann Davis[18]

St. James College
January 3d 1858

Dear Ma

I arrived here safely Thursday evening about six oclock. There were two other boys besides myself, and as we thought the stage would be pretty full we concluded to take a carriage, we got one for ten dollars. When I got to the Fredrick junction I did not think about Mr Huttons box, and when I got to Fredrick it was not there, but it came up in the stage the next day. Dr. Kerfoot said yesterday that there were several boys in the College study who were not sixteen and that he intended to put them down in the Grammar school. I do not know whether he will put me there or not I hope not. Dr. Kerfoot has not said any thing to me about my music yet.

Give my love to all

---

[17] *Register of the College of St. James, 1858*, 7. See Skardon, 68.

[18] WWD to HAD, 3 January 1858, ABD Letters.

> Your devoted Son
> Wilkins Davis

When arround the merry table
Think of those who've none
The orphan and the widowed
The hungry and alone.
Bountiful your offerings to the altar bring
And let the poor an needy a Christmas carol sing.
Chor. Carol brothers carol
    Carol joyfully
    Carol brothers carol
    Carol merrily
And sing a gladsome Christmas
To all good christian men
Carol brothers carol
Christmas day again.
N.B. The above is part of a hymn sung by us Christmas morning.

> W Davis

During Holy Week each year the usual pattern of school events changed considerably. Some studies were laid aside--Caesar, Virgil, Xenophon--and others taken up in their place: students were required to memorize, in Latin, the Creeds, the *Te Deum*, the *Pater Noster*, and various ancient hymns. They read parts of the New Testament in Greek and, instead of the usual work in algebra or geometry, were instructed in the history and use of the church calendar. There were extra chapel services during the week and special lectures on such subjects as the destruction of Jerusalem, the prophecies of Daniel, and the history of sacrifice.[19]

W. Wilkins Davis to Allen Bowie Davis[20]

St. James College
April 2d 1858

Dear Pa,

I have just recieved your letter conveighing the sad inteligence of poor Henrys death. I never knew untill this moment how I may say I really loved him I feel as if I had lost a friend and my eyes are so full of tears that I can scarcely see to write. I trust he had made his peace with God before he died, his is one of the many cases which are happening every day to forwarn us of our future end for no one knows whose turn will come next nor can any too soon become a disciple of Christ. This day was the lamb of sinners crucified to attone for the sins of the world. This week being holy week we have had some

---

[19] Coit, "Recollections," 353-54.

[20] WWD to ABD, 2 April 1858, ABD Letters.

change in our studies instead of our usual lesson in Greek we have been reading the betrayal and crucifiction of our Lord from a Greek Testament. We have had chapel six times a day this week, two times voluntary and one a lecture from Dr. K[erfoot] on the history of the prayer book. We have had a sermon every day and some of them as good as I would wish to hear especially Dr Kerfoots sermons.

Our holiday will be on the (14. 15. 16.th.) of April. Tell Ma I hope she will remain that long in Baltimore as I should like to go their very much to spend my holidays, if she remains that long please let me know, and tell Ma to have sister Beck in town at that time.

>Give my love to all
>Your affectionate and
>devoted Son
>Wilkins Davis

In June of 1858 Hester Ann Davies wrote her son about the significance of Confirmation:

> You seem to think that I would be glad to have you a Christian. I would indeed be very glad if as a family we could all be consistent Christians. The rite of Confirmation is a very solemn one. It involves mighty and momentous responsibilities. It is making a public profession of religion, and taking a vow that henceforth

you will renounce and resist all sin public or private, secret or open, and henceforth are resolved to lead a new life, keeping all Gods commandments, and walking devoutly in his ways, renouncing all dependanse on the flesh, but living in the Spirit. Taking up Christ's cross, and never to be ashamed on any occasion to be pointed at as one of his disciples. "Except a man be born again" be changed by the operation of the Spirit on his heart so that his affections from being wholly fixed on earthly things are elevated, purified and placed on God, and be made <u>meet</u> and <u>prepared</u> for heaven he cannot enter into heaven. The Scripture says he must truly repent, he must be sorry for his sins.... Do you feel a strong desire to obtain the forgiveness of your sins, are you in prayer pleading for a new heart and the indwelling of Gods Holy Spirit. Are you resolved at every sacrifice to devote yourself ... to the service of your Creator then I can have no objection to your being confirmed and becoming a communicant. But I would not like you lightly to assume such a vow. The mere hasty resolve in <u>your own strength</u>, with the laying on of the Bishops hands, cannot impart it. It must be the gift of the Spirit, and it can only be obtained by earnest faithful intercession, trusting only in Christ's merits and intercessions. Write me your own views, I should be glad if they are of the most serious character. We cannot think about the value of our souls too soon, and our decision determines our future destiny. It is either hell or heaven. Our conduct in our present state of probation will fix forever our fate. The Bible says "Remember your Creator in the days of youth." There cannot be more favorable time before evil habits are confirmed and riveted. I hope you will give this matter your prayerful attention. If you feel no interest in religious things and it is a matter of indifference I would not decide hastily.[21]

Wilkins answered his mother in the letter below. The instructor he refers to who had recently been made a deacon was undoubtedly John Kerfoot Lewis, ordained on 30 May 1858 by Bishop Whittingham. The Irving Society, mentioned in the postscript, sponsored essay contests, debates, orations, and similar acitivities--whatever might fulfill its intention to be a "valuable auxiliary in forming a correct literary taste." Its moderator at this time was Joseph H. Coit, professor of physics and natural history. Washington Irving, who allowed the group to use his name after "the Philomathean Society" failed to gain widespread acceptance, also gave the students a device (the holly leaf) and a motto (*sub sole, sub umbre virens*) to use on their banner. In 1858 Irving Society speakers addressed such topics as the power of the press, imperialism and France, "unwritten poetry," and John C. Calhoun.[22] The bishop

---

[21] HAD to WWD, June [1858], ABD Letters.

[22] *Calendar of the Irving Society of the College of St. James, ... 1848 to ... 1860* (Baltimore, [1860]), 14-20, 22-27; *Register of the College of St. James, 1858*, 23-24; *Register of the College of St. James, 1859*, 24.

mentioned was Thomas March Clark (1812-1903). He was a natural choice for a speaker. One of the first clergymen to discard the old-fashioned preaching style, he addressed his listeners in a straightforward, often witty, manner. Only a few years before he had published a series of his lectures to young men, *Early Discipline and Culture* (1855).[23]

W. Wilkins Davis to Hester Ann Davis[24]

> St. James College
> June 13th 1858

Dear Ma,

    I recieved your letter last night together with one from Ester, and the night before I recieved one from Sister Beck together with the bundle you sent me.

    I hope you will not for an instant think that I would be confirmed without giving it my most earnest and devout

---

[23] Mary Clark Sturtevant, *Thomas March Clark, Fifth Bishop of Rhode Island: A Memoir* (Milwaukee, 1927); *Dictionary of American Biography*, s.v. "Clark, Thomas March."

[24] WWD to HAD, 13 June 1858, ABD Letters.

attention. I have thought upon it long and well, and I have prayed to my maker for his Son's sake, that I may meet the comming period (when I hope by my almighty's grace to become one of his deciples), with strength due to repentance. I think as the 29th article of religion says that any person partaking of the sacrament (as I will be permitted to do if I am confirmed) not with a lively faith, partakes of so great a thing to his condemnation.

I cannot say that I am prepared for confirmation, but hope by the Grace of God to be prepared by commencement. Dr. Kerfoot has promised me that I shall have the benefit of his prayers and advice. I expect that Dr. Kerfoot will very soon form a class of all those who wish to be confirmed. One of our instructors was Ordained a Deacon last Sunday week, he preached his first sermon last Sunday which I think was a very good one for a beginning.

>
> Give my love to all
> Your devoted Son
> Wilkins Davis

P.S. Our school breaks up on the 14th of July. The Irving Society intend having their sixth biennial celebration on Wednesday next. Rt. Rev. Dr. Clark of Rhode Island is to deliver the address.

>
> Wilkins Davis

The following letter begins with a brief mention of a subject that would in time become a real interest of Wilkins's--science. The "Dr. Steiner" he names was Lewis Henry Steiner, M.D. (1827-1892), who, as a young man, decided he would rather teach science than practice medicine. From 1854 to 1859 he was a lecturer on physics and chemistry at the College of St. James. Later he taught at the Maryland Institute, the Maryland College of Pharmacy, and elsewhere. During the Civil War he became chief inspector in the U.S. Sanitary Commission, attached to the Army of the Potomac. After the war he served in the state senate and became the first librarian of the Enoch Pratt Free Library.[25] Wilkins gives below a brief description of part of his school day. The schedule at the College of St. James was similar to the schedule at Muhlenberg's St. Paul's College.[26] Students enjoyed one or two hours of recreation in the afternoons and spent the rest of their waking hours at meals, in chapel (attendance at Morning Prayer and Evening Prayer was mandatory; the service at noon was voluntary), and at study.[27] The alumni award was for

---

[25] Scharf, *History of Western Maryland* 2:1240; 1:488; Richard H. Hart, *Lewis Henry Steiner and his Son Bernard Christian Steiner* (n.p., 1936), 1-3; *Appleton's Cyclopedia*, s.v. "Steiner, Lewis Henry"; *Biographical Cyclopedia of Representative Men of Maryland and the District of Columbia*, 616-17; *Who Was Who in America*, Historical Volume 1607-1896, rev. ed., s.v. "Steiner, Lewis Henry."

[26] See Skardon, 73.

[27] Coit, "Recollections," 338.

exactly those accomplishments described by Wilkins in his letter; the contest was held every year, Latin alternating with Greek as the language on which students were tested.[28] John W. Breathed acted as the bursar at St. James's. His official titles were Secretary of the College and Curator for the Students. The "Mrs. Porter" referred to was Mrs. Mary E. Porter, who ran a school for girls in Brookeville. Ingleside Seminary (founded in 1845) was "a Home School for Young Ladies" near Catonsville in Baltimore County. The students there attended St. Timothy's Episcopal Church on Sundays. Rebecca Dorsey Davis was an 1861 Graduate.[29]

---

[28]*Proceedings of the Sixth Annual meeting of the Association of the Alumni of the College of St. James ... 1858*, 4-8; *Register of the College of St. James, 1859* (Baltimore, 1859), 22-23.

[29] Scharf, *History of Western Maryland*, 2:1259; Bowie, 202; *Ingleside Seminary: Founded 1845. A Home School for Young Ladies; Near Catonsville, Baltimore County, MD* (Baltimore, 1859), 7, 8, 13; *Ingleside Seminary: Founded 1845 ...* (Baltimore, 1873), 4. After the war Breathed moved to Virginia and became mayor of Lynchburg. One of his sons, James Breathed, served with distinction as an artillery officer in the confederate army. See Williams, 365-66.

W. Wilkins Davis to Allen Bowie Davis[30]

St. James College
October 10th. 1858.

Dear Pa,

I received your letter last night, together with the check, which I gave to Mr Breathed. I have not yet given the stone to Dr. Kerfoot, and I am afraid it will be difficult to get the necessary aparatus, so that I think if you are not in a hurry for it I had better keep it untill Dr. Steiner comes up next Spring, he is one of the best Chemists in the state. The Washington County Agricultural Fair commences next Thursday and lasts two days. I expect all the boys will go over there either on Thursday or Friday. I expect to see Cousin Richard [Johns] Bowie there if I go. I wish you would come up there I know you would be delighted with it, you would also have an opportunity of seeing this College, which I know you very much desire.

I wrote a letter to Sister Beck last Sunday and received one from her on Tuesday last which I have answered.

We rise at twenty minutes past five and get through breakfast about half past six, when we have an interval of thirty

---

[30] WWD to ABD, 10 October 1858, ABD Letters.

minutes before the regular duties of the day commence during which time I take a walk of about a mile and a half or two miles, or play a game of bandy which gives me plenty of physical exercise.

My studies this year are Virgil which we have nearly finished, Homer, English Composition, Geometry, Algebra, History, and French, which studies combined, give abundance of exercise to my intellectual powers. The Alumni have offered a premium of 50 Dollars to the boy who will be able to read any part of the first four books of the Annals of Tacitus fluently, and answer the most difficult questions upon them which a committee of seven can put, and to write a Latin thesis the subject of which shall be "De Caesaris Morte." As Tacitus is studied by the Senoir Class, the contest lies only between the select of the Junior and Senior Classes.

Tell Essy if she studies hard and learns her lessons well by the time Mrs Porter commences she will be able to keep the head of the class, and by the time she goes to Engleside she will be able to get along without any trouble, but if she is lazy, (like I was at Brookeville, and Mr Prentises,) she will always regret it hereafter because she will have to study so much harder. The College appears to be hard up for money this year in consequence of which we have not quite so good a table as last year.

Give my love to all

>Your devoted Son
>W. Wilkins Davis

The letters of Wilkins's parents were full of advice for their son. Wilkins's remarks above having to do with his recreational activity were a response to his father's urging him in a letter Wilkins had probably just received to develop habits of daily exercise.[31] Several days later Mrs. Davis wrote to her son to remind him of all the reasons people have to be humble, asking him to consider the work of the Creator, "a powerful, wise, and inscrutable being whose ways are past finding out."[32] On 29 October Allen Bowis Davis wrote Wilkins, stating

> I hope you still keep up your habit of exercise and early rising. It will be of great advantage to you to lay the foundation of a vigorous and robust frame at your present time of life. Any bad habits or overindulgence you allow while you are growing so fast will be hard to get rid of. You must fight against them and <u>conquer yourself</u>. Self indulgence is the most formidable enemy a young man has to encounter.... No man ever rose to goodness and eminence who did not obtain a victory over his evil habits and inclinations....

---

[31] ABD to WWD, 7 October 1858, ABD Letters.

[32] HAD to WWD, 14 October 1858, ABD Letters.

> Read attentively and carefully and prayerfully the Proverbs of Solomon. They contain a world of wisdom which ought to be indelliably written on the heart of every young man.[33]

The parents' letters combined moral and educational counsel with sometimes heavy doses of theology. Hester Ann Davis wrote Wilkins that she had met in Mechanicsville (probably at St. John's Church) a "young Mr. Coleburn," a graduate of the College of St. James, and that he had advanced a

> sacramental theory of grace through the ministry in the administration of the sacraments. But it seems to me so much more rational and so easy to go immediately by faith "to the fountain filled with blood," wash and be cleansed, nor can I see the slightest warrant for it in the Scriptures. It seems to me always to indicate a very, very low state of Christian experience. If we would seek an acquaintance with God by earnest prayer, which we must, and if he as he did to Moses, would put us in the rock, and pass by revealing himself to us as the Lord God Merciful and gracious forgiving iniquity, transgression and sin, we would cast our sacramental remissions to the moles and the bats. I revere the sacraments but only as outward signs and seals of the inward and spiritual grace, only to be obtained by

---

[33] ABD to WWD, 29 October 1858, ABD Letters.

simple faith, or an implicit reliance on the atonement made for our sins by our Saviors blood-shedding. The fruit of this faith is <u>internal peace</u>. We are still poor, needy, helpless, sinners, or very inconsistent Christians but sin is not imputed to us, because our faith just like Abrahams is imputed to us for righteousness. Now do not be discouraged by your sinfulness. Do not look at your sins, look to Jesus the Author and finisher of faith, and ask him to work this faith in you, and you will find your light and strength increasing more and more until the perfect day. Break off from every sin at once. You will never find it easier.... I cannot consent to your stopping French. You have time and talent to do French and drawing justice all in good time.... Do be very quiet and gentlemanly.[34]

Wilkins came home to Greenwood for a short break at Christmas. When he returned to St. James's he took with him, according to his mother's diary, "a large box, containing ham, turkey, 5 kinds of cake, five mince pies, <u>84</u> sausages and a quantity of biscuits."[35]

As the second half of the term began at the College, Allen Bowie Davis wrote his son to convey more advice. Wilkins has "left off French" and "promised Dr. Kerfoot to be

---

[34] HAD to WWD, 11 November 1858, ABD Letters.

[35] HAD diary, [December 1858].

more diligent in your other studies in consideration of this relief." Mr. Davis hoped his son would acquire the "habit of close application and hard study" that the father was never taught at Brookeville. "You have much greater advantages for improvement than I ever enjoyed and I hope and believe you will reap a rich reward for it." Davis said he was glad Wilkins had preserved and committed to his mother's keeping some of her excellent letters to him. He adjured his son "never [to] loose them or forget the excellent advice ... she has so beautifully given you. You are fortunate my son in having such a mother. Few boys have so great a blessing. Return to her love, respect, obedience...."[36] After receiving in February the monthly report on Wilkins's progress Allen Bowie Davis wrote: "You have a few disorder marks, of which we want to see as few as possible."[37] The next day he wrote again to say he had spoken with Mr. Richard Hutton, who "says you are improving in your Greek and habits of application." Since Wilkins has dropped French he should now be able to give not only "evidence of <u>improvement</u> in your other studies, but of complete success in mastering them. You are now nearly seventeen and if you do not now acquire a habit of close application and a determination to surmount every difficulty, you never will."[38]

---

[36] ABD to WWD, 14 January 1859, ABD Letters.

[37] ABD to WWD, 11 February 1859, ABD Letters.

[38] ABD to WWD, 12 February 1859, ABD Letters.

Wilkins enjoyed music; his instrument was the flute. On 14 March 1859 Hester Ann Davis wrote in her diary that

> Wilkins father gave him only a year since a handsome flute, which cost $19. He know wants another at $30, having broken his. His father does not much relish this. I wrote him today I had expatiated largely on all his meritorious qualities, presented in bold relief the various sins young people are prone to commit, which he had been so wise or so lucky as to avoid. Painted him so over as to make him look like a whited sepulchre, but said nothing about the <u>bones within</u>. The end of the conference was, <u>I suppose he must have it</u>.[39]

Mrs. Davis was upset with her son a month later for ordering from a gift store two books (which he gave to the school's Belles Lettres Society), a set of gold studs, and a gold pencil with an ivory handle (which he intended to present to Rebecca). Twenty boys came after him for the gift store's address when they espied Wilkins's merchandise. Hester Ann Davis commented in her diary, "I am sorry for this...."[40]

---

[39] HAD diary, 14 March 1859.

[40] HAD diary, 13 April [1859]. Wilkins was a member of the Belles Lettres society, a literary and debating group similar to the Irving Society. He is listed as a member of the Committee of Invitation that sent out announcements of the Society's tenth annual celebration. Printed invitation, 22 June 1859, ABD Papers, Box 1.

Students at the College of St. James sat for examinations at three points in the school year: before Christmas, before Easter, and at midsummer. They were tested on the work of the previous three months.[41] Wilkins had just finished his Easter exams when he wrote the letter below. The matron he mentions was Mrs. Eliza Chauncy Clark Porter, mother of a man who would become well known during the Civil War as a general in the Union army, Fitz-John Porter, and grandmother of Lucian Porter Waddell, an instructor at the College and Fitz-John Porter's nephew.[42]

W. Wilkins Davis to Rebecca Dorsey Davis[43]

St. James College
April 19th. 1859

Dear Sister,

I received your letter a week ago, and fully intended answering it before but I have been so much engaged that I

---

[41] *Register of the College of St. James, 1858*, 20.

[42] *The New England Historical and Genealogical Register* 11 (April 1857): 148-52; Harrison, *Life of Kerfoot* 1:212. Harrison states that Mrs. Porter "was a lovely and accomplished woman."

[43] WWD to RDD, 19 April 1859, ABD Letters.

really had not time, an you must excuse me. Taking it for granted that this letter will find you at Barnums[44] I direct there. One week from to day we have our long looked for private celebration. I guess if it is clear Hagerstown will be pretty well represented. The morning after our celebration I expect to leave here little after four for Baltimore. Our examination passed off very nicely. John B. [Kerfoot] says it is the best one we've had for some time. I passed decidedly the best examination I have passed since I have been here, and was decidedly more lucky for I was only called upon in one thing oraly and I got nine for that. I guess I got pretty good marks in my written examination also but the marks will not be read out untill next Monday.

Mr. Dick Hutton is turning out a flaming pair of whiskers. I thought of turning out mine, but his grew so fast that mine got frightened and concluded to wait awhile. Mr. Dick, also, has got the chicken pox which he has been so condescending as to hand over to me, and consequently I am pepered with little red spots from head to foot. Mr. Breathed and Dr. Kerfoot say it is the chicken pox, but Mrs. Porter, the matron says it is the rash and gave me a dose of magnesia on the strength of it. It does not make much matter to me which of the two diseases it is neither of them are of any account except that they itch a little now and then. I should like to

---

[44] Barnum's City Hotel was at the corner of Rayette and Calvert Streets in Baltimore. It opened in 1825 and closed in 1889.

know what you took it upon yourself to inform them at home that I was thin for, the boys do say I look like a bean pole with a turnip sticking on the top, but that was no cause for your alarming them at home, and also getting me a lecture from Dr. K. Whether I have fallen off or not you shall have the pleasure of seeing yourself in a day or two. April 20th. I received a letter from you last night. I am very sorry that you should be disapointed at my nonappearance tomorrow, but Dr. K. would no more think of letting me spend a week in Baltimore, than he would of flying. He thinks I have lost enough time already. I hope Pa will write to him this week, then, perhaps, he might let me stay a day longer, but at anrate you need look for me before next Wednesday, at which time I expect your holidays will be nearly over. We are carrying things to the top of the ladder here this week (passion week.) We have chapel five times a day, a lecture in the afternoon on the origin of the prayer book, and also, instead of our regular lesson we have to translate the gospel of St. John from a greek testament, (10 verses a day,) then we have a long latin hymn to translate and commit to memory, and in mathematics we are learning to find out when Easter and the other moveable feasts of the church come.

    Give my love to Ma and Pa
    W. Wilkins Davis.

P.S. If Pa did not receive my last letter before leaving home, please tell him that Dr. K. wont receive any application for leave of absence through the students, and ask him please to write to Dr. K. himself.

W. Davis

In May, Hester Ann Davis took Wilkins to task in a humorous fashion for his lack of "chivalrous courtesy" toward the young ladies of Hagerstown. "We are somewhat amused at your <u>pretended</u> antipathy to the fair sex." She assured him that "It is certainly written in the book of Fate, that at a certain hour, on a certain day, ... you shall be pierced to the heart ... by an arrow from the unerring hand of that pitiless tyrant Cupid. To which one and all say <u>Amen</u>."[45] As this passage indicates, Wilkins's parents were not always solemn and censorious. Had they been so, they probably would not have allowed their daughter Mary to have a pet lamb, which, this same month, was eating strawberry plants, cropping off the shrubbery, running through Greenwood's parlors, and soiling the carpets.[46] Family members clearly enjoyed one another's company on those occasions when they could be together. On the evening of the day in mid July that Wilkins returned home from the College of St. James he accompanied his sisters Mary and Rebecca on the flute while they sang--"very touchingly," their

---

[45] HAD to WWD, 18 May 1859, ABD Letters.

[46] HAD diary, 20 May 1859.

mother felt--and played the piano. "We are to day a happy and united family," Hester Ann Davis observed.[47]

Mrs. Davis could be critical of her son: on Tuesday, 19 July 1859, she "made Wilkins come into my room and read with me Shakspear. He reads very humdrum and has no style whatever--not the slightest variation in manner, of enunciation or tones of voice."[48] But of course her criticism was rooted in concern for his well-being. When it was time for him to start his sophomore year at the College of St. James she was full of regret: "Poor Wilkins left this morning for St. James. I could have wept bitterly. I could have shut myself in my chamber absorbed in grief, but I thought it most Christian to meet with fortitude, a seperation which is unavoidable, and absolutely necessary to his future welfare."[49] As the months wore on, her anxiety about Wilkins's progress became mixed with her anxiety over the course of the nation. She wrote her son on 28 October of John Brown and other abolitionists: "I see no possibility, not a ray of hope, of the conversion of those fanatics. It has actually become a compound part of their religion. But I think they are acting a very shabby part. After abetting and aiding his treasonable and murderous designs, in the hour of his adversity they have forsaken him, and are too

---

[47] HAD diary, 14 July 1859.

[48] HAD diary, 19 July 1859.

[49] HAD diary, 28 September 1859.

cowardly to pay counsel to defend him." Brown she regarded as "evidently an extraordinary man" who might have become a better person had he enjoyed the advantages of early education and developed his good points and restrained his bad. "Pray my dear child for grace to curb and control your evil propensities. Cherish neither envy, malice, hatred nor revenge.... You are called to act on the stage of life, at a remarkable period of its history. You will truly need all the wisdom, caution, and prudence of an astute philosopher to cope with those around you. I feel very uneasy about the state of the Country. If the abolitionists continue their nefarious efforts, we may never know when we may not expect a mine to spring in our midst."[50]

In November she wrote Wilkins that "Poor Brown is convicted. I really cannot think him so awfully wicked as some do. He had become a man of one idea ... a monomaniac." She asked him how he was faring in mathematics and said she had heard that Dr. Coaklay "shows partiality to some boys, those who happen to displease him he neglects. How do you stand with him."[51] George W. Coaklay (1814-1893) was professor of mathematics, analytical mechanics, and astronomy at the College from 1840 to 1860.[52] Hester Ann Davis urged Wilkins

---

[50] HAD to WWD, 28 [October] 1859, ABD Letters.

[51] HAD to WWD, 3 November 1859, ABD Letters.

[52] *Register of the College of St. James ... for ... 1850-51*, 7; Scharf, *History of Western Maryland* 2:1240; *Twentieth Century Biographical Dictionary of*

to practice his flute regularly and to "shun <u>sloth</u> and <u>procrastination</u>."[53] To fortify her son for the task ahead, she sent him back to the College of St. James after a brief Christmas recess with a box containing a turkey, a ham, seventy-two sausages, fifty-three biscuits, a loaf of bread, a sponge cake, some ginger pound cakes, and some crisp ginger bread. She noted in her diary that he now stood six feet, two inches in height.[54]

A month after his return to the College she wrote to tell him "I am glad you had 9 for your composition at Christmas. But your industry is only 8 your decorum 7 and 6 disorder marks. I hope you will try to be the <u>gentleman</u> as well as the <u>scholar</u>."[55] Disorder marks were given for such offenses as being absent from class (one or two marks), lateness (one each minute tardy), and disorder in class (one or more depending on the extent of the disruption). They could affect a student's honors but did not carry any other penalty unless they exceeded a certain number. Earlier in the College's history, harsher penalties were inflicted on misbehaving students, who might have been whipped (grammar school boys only) or

---

Notable Americans, s.v. "Coakley, George Washington." His name also appears, in other sources, as "Coaklay."

[53] HAD to WWD, 3 November 1859, ABD Letters.

[54] HAD diary, 27, 28 December 1859.

[55] HAD to WWD, 26 [January] 1860, ABD Letters.

confined for several hours in a lock-up and given only bread and water.[56]

W. Wilkins Davis to Rebecca Dorsey Davis[57]

St. James College
Feb. 29th. 1860

Dear Sister,

I received your letter last night. I think you have rather a mistaken idea about novels, for if you carefully peruse the light reading of any country, you will in nineteen cases out of twenty get a better knowledge of it than you could from regular history. This may at first seen very strange, but when you come out that nearly all histories heretofore written, were written for party purposes, you can see through it at once. Take Macaulay for instance the very man whose work you are reading. He is a most notorious story teller, and no reliance is to be placed in him at all. He was a blind adherent of the Whig party, and would say nothing which would injure his party, while on the other hand he would not hestitate to overstep the bounds of truth if he could by that means injure the Tories. I think

---

[56] *Register of the College of St. James, 1858*, 21; Coit, "Recollections," 341.

[57] WWD to RDD, 29 February 1860, ABD Letters.

Warren Hastings was a Tory, and I venture to say, Macaulay says everything he can against him, and that he fully deserved impeachment.[58] Now such works as Keats and Shakespeare's if properly read will give you an insight into facts concerning different courts and nations, which are both interesting and important, yet slured over by the historian as to insignifcant to notice. Dont think from this that I would not advise you to read history, I think every one ought to do so; but I do not think light reading is to be past over as worthless and uninstructive.

In our English Literature yesterday we were studying about the "Mediaeval Drama." In speaking of those in the Middle Ages, one is mentioned on the Creation, in one of the scenes of which, Cain and Abel are brought up by their father before the Almighty to be examined on the Lords Prayer. Abel got through very well, only had to be prompted two or three times, but Cain being rather inclined to be stubborn, refused to take his hat offe, whereupon his father boxed his jaws, and then being urged on by the devil who stood behind him, he said the prayer backwards and got a sound thrashing for his trouble. In another piece a prize is offered to the man who can tell the biggest falsehood. Four men come forward, a pedlar, a pilgrim,

---

[58] Warren Hastings (1732-1818) was the first governor general of British India. He resigned from this post in 1784 and returned to England, where he was impeached in 1787 on charges that included extortion, responsibility for judicial murder, and the hiring out of British troops to local rulers. His trial, which began in 1788, ended in acquittal in 1795.

a politicary, and a pardoner: after a good deal of astonishing mendacity the pardoner asserts, as if by accident, that he never saw a woman out of temper; and this being unanimously agreed to be the greatest lie ever heard, the prize is awarded to the assertor of so tremendous a falsehood.

>   Give my love to Marie.
>   Your devoted Brother
>   W. Wilkins Davis

On 30 March Mrs. Davis wrote Wilkins and conveyed her wish that he "profit by [his] present advantages." He could never again "expect such complete isolation from care, anxiety, intrusion, the duties of life, temptations to indolence and the calls of pleasure as you do at present...." She reminded him that "the impression favorable or unfavorable which you make at college must to a considerable extent influence your future public character." She asked him to work hard for her sake as well as his: "I will not be so unreasonable as to say nothing short of the first honors in you class will satisfy me, but I should be mortified if you be left to lag in the rear. It would be a reflection on my character. Aspasia history tells us made Pericles, Cornelia the Gracchi, and it has been long patent that smart men always had superior mothers. Then my child for your own sake, for my sake, be reasonably diligent in study and circumspect in action." She concluded by asking him to bring home his linen coat and standing collars and told him he would soon meet some of Rebecca's friends --"you must now be something of the <u>beau</u>."[59]

W. Wilkins Davis to Rebecca Dorsey Davis[60]

St. James College
May 8th. 1860

Dear Sister,

I have just received your letter, and it gives me great delight to hear that you think of being confirmed. I should advise you, by all means, so to do, unless you feel yourself totaly unfit to receive that solemn rite, and unworthy to partake of the blessed body and blood of our Savior Jesus Christ. It is indeed a dreadful thing to receive the Holy Communion unworthily, and I fear we poor mortals are too prone to underrate the great privilege granted to us, but if we confess our sins before our Maker with a lowly and penitent heart, he will not fail to give us his grace to withstand the temptations of the world, the flesh, and the devil. I would not

---

[59] HAD to WWD, 30 March 1860, ABD Letters. Cornelia was the mother of the Gracchi and Aspasia the mistress of Pericles.

[60] WWD to RDD, 8 May 1860, ABD Letters.

advise you to hesitate about coming to a decision, but to make up your mind to it and pray to God to give you his grace through his son Jesus Christ, ever keeping in mind the blessed promises he has made to those who faithfully serve him in this life.

I do not look upon the medical profession as any thing dreadfull at all, indeed I think, the holy ministry being excepted, it is the highest profession a man can follow. Just as your letter came I finished a small treatise on Physiology and Animal Mechanism. I found it so interesting that I procured another book on the same subject which I intend to commence tomorrow. One of the boys the other day gave me a fish the other day, which though the knife was very dull, I succeeded in desecting pretty well. I took out the eyes and showed the optic nerve, the various coats, humors, etc. of the bull to an admiring crowd. I really have two teeth which want pluging very bad.

> Give my love to Marie
> Your devoted brother
> W. W. Davis

In the middle of May, Allen Bowie Davis wrote his son and said that his body was suffering (inflamed eye, acid stomach, and irritated legs) but the farm was doing well: the wheat was good and the corn never looked better. He also mentioned that he had attended the convention of the Constitutional Union party (held in Baltimore on 9 May) and was favorably impressed with the speeches and patriotic spirit he had witnessed there: "I can most cordially support the ticket. If elected it will do credit to any party or nation."[61]

W. Wilkins Davis to Hester Ann Davis[62]

St. James College
June 3d. 1860

Dear Ma,

I received your letter on Wednesday last and am much obliged for the money you sent. I should have liked very much to have gotten you some nice little cases to put in your cabinet, but Hagerstown is such a one horse kind of a place that I was unable to get anything better than cigar boxes. I have got some beautiful and rare bugs, moths etc. Just commencing as I am, and never having seen anything of the kind before, I cant succeed very well at first, but I am beginning to get my hand as the saying is, and become somewhat acquainted with the ways to preserve the insects. I am unable to find any work about

---

[61] ABD to WWD, 18 May 1860, ABD Letters.

[62] WWD to HAD, 3 June 1860, ABD Letters.

here from which I can learn how to classify, and arrainge my specimens in the most Entomological manner, and if Pa should have an opportunity of seeing the Entomologist at the Patent Office or any other one, I would be very much obliged if he would ask him what work I could get that would teach me how to arrainge them.

I am now reading the first two volumes of the Bridgewater Treatises on the power, wisdom, and goodness of God, as manifested in the Creation. These only give a general view of the History, habits, and instincts of animals. These Bridgewater Treatises are very fine works, and I would advise you to buy them if you get any books. One of them on the Hand by Sir Charles Bell M.D. I have heard spoken of as one of the finest productions in the English language, and would like to read it very much.[63]

---

[63] Sir Charles Bell's book *The Hand, its Mechanism and Vital Endowments, as Evincing Design* was first published in 1833 in London as the fourth of the famous Bridgewater Treatises. It subsequently went through many editions and was published in Philadelphia, Utrecht, Stuttgart, and New York. The volumes in this series appeared, ironically, during the period of young Charles Darwin's voyage on the naval survey vessel H.M.S. *Beagle*. All the treatises were subtitled *On the Power, Wisdom and Goodness of God as Manifested in the Creation*. Their point was to demonstrate, along the lines of the natural theology of Joseph Butler (1692-1752) and William Paley (1743-1805), the reasonableness of Christianity; the Bridgewater books tried to supply scientific evidence for a teleological argument for God's existence. The orderliness and design of the world were held to reveal divine purpose. Of course, on Darwin's view, the natural process of biological development contained no hint of intelligence or purpose, let alone any proof of divine benevolence. Darwin's writings, which were just starting to appear at the time WWD was a student at St. James's, soon overwhelmed the testimony of men like Bell; or, to put it more accurately, treatises such as Bell's came to

I have just learned from Dr. Kerfoot that Pa was not at the convention, and fear very much that he was sick.[64] Pleas let me know how he is.

Give my love to all.
Your devoted Son.
W.W. Davis

P.S. As I principally rely on getting my butterflies and moths from cocoons and crysalises, you may save all that the children may happen to find. All the caterpillers, grubworms etc. I find I put in a box and feed so as to obtain the cocoons etc.

W.W. Davis

Monday 4th. I have just this moment stumbled on a Smithsonian report which gives some instructions on collecting insects, the one for 1858. I see that succeeding reports will have something on the subjects. If you have them please take care of them.[65]

---

be read in the light of Darwinism and were found to include valuable details corroborative of evolutionary theory. See Gordon Gordon-Taylor and E. W. Walls, *Sir Charles Bell: His Life and Times* (Edinburgh and London, 1958), 163-65.

[64] The diocesan convention was held on 30-31 May 1860 at Christ Church in Baltimore.

[65] The report Wilkins had in mind was "Instructions for Collecting Insects," in *Annual Report of the Board of Regents of the Smithsonian Institution ... for*

When Wilkins returned to Greenwood in July, he brought with him, his mother noted, "a beautiful collection of butter flies and insects, bugs etc."[66]

In November John Barrett Kerfoot visited the Brookeville area and preached at St. Bartholomew's. Allen Bowie Davis wrote Wilkins that "Dr. Kerfoots visit has been a most agreeable one to us, and he has made a most favorable impression both for himself and the College." Kerfoot raised almost four hundred dollars on this trip, including $250 from Davis himself. A. B. Davis commented "I do not see how the College can fail under a Priest so energetic, wise and prudent as he appears to be."[67]

... *1858*, U.S. Senate, 35th Cong., 2d sess., Miscellaneous Document no. 49 (Washington, 1859), 158-200.

[66] HAD diary, 12 July 1860.

[67] ABD to WWD, November 1860, ABD Letters; HAD diary, [November] 1860.

W. Wilkins Davis to Rebecca Dorsey Davis[68]

St. James College
Novem. 14th. 1860

Dear Sister,

I received your letter last night. We took the defeat of Bell pretty cooly, as, dignified student like we are, or consider ourselves to be, ought to take everything.[69]

I am begining to enjoy myself pretty sharp by this time, although I have to work uncommon hard. Three of us have formed ourselves into a scientific and medical board. As a scientific board we intend to establish a laboratory if Dr. Kerfoot will permit us to have the chemicals. I fear though that he will be afraid of our blowing ourselves and everything

---

[68] WWD to RDD, 14 November 1860, ABD Letters.

[69] In the 1860 presidential election Abraham Lincoln, Republican, finished first with 1,866,000 popular votes, followed by Stephen A. Douglas, Democrat (Northern), with 1,383,000, John C. Breckinridge, Democrat (Southern), with 848,000, and John Bell, Constitutional Unionist, with 593,000. The voting pattern of Marylanders, however, was quite different from that of Americans as a whole. In Maryland the contest was exclusively between Bell and Breckinridge. The latter took the state's eight electoral votes with a popular vote of 42,282 (45.8%). Bell came in second with 41,760 (45.2), followed at a considerable distance by Douglas 5,966 (6.5) and Lincoln 2,294 (2.5). In Montgomery County, Bell narrowly bested Breckinridge; there the vote was Bell 1,155 (47.6%), Breckinridge 1,125 (46.3), Douglas 99 (4.1), and Lincoln 50 (2.0). Evitts, 150.

else to pieces. The medical board holds a consultation whenever a subject can be procured, such as a rat, cat, rabbit, etc. We tried to buy a puppy for our next consultation, but the owner was unwilling to part with him. We generally put an end to our subjects with sulphurous acid, but if we get our chemicals we will administer other substances detrimental to life. We dont look upon this as at all cruel, but all for the advancement of science. We have also another association, composed of a friend, my room mate, and myself. It is called the ginger bread association. My room mate and myself send in every other Saturday and buy a lot of ginger bread to eat on Sunday. On the intermediate Saturday, the other member buys the ginger bread.

Dr. Kerfoot went to our house last Saturday. I am sure he gave a good account of me, for I have been studying very hard lately and got nines throughout last week.

Give my love to Marrie and Essie.

> Your devoted brother
> W. W. Davis

In the following letter Wilkins urges his mother and father not to become too hopeful with respect to his taking a second "testimonial." Testimonials were "rewards of excellence in scholarship and conduct" conferred according to three grades of distinction by the bishop (on the recommendation of the faculty) at the commencement ceremony every July. Testimonials and the Alumni Prize in the Greek and Latin Languages were the school's principal honors.[70] Wilkins also mentions below the possibility of his teaching in a Sunday school Kerfoot might soon establish in the area. It appears to have been common practice for persons affiliated with the College of St. James to serve in local churches. Faculty members who were also priests--e.g., Joseph C. Passmore, Alexander Falk, and Joseph H. Coit--frequently held rectorships or supplied at St. Mark's (Lappans Crossroad) and other nearby churches.

W. Wilkins Davis to Allen Bowie Davis[71]

St. James College
Nov. 25th. 1860

Dear Pa,

I suppose the inclement weather we have had last week, has driven all idea of your western tour, for the present at least,

---

[70] *Commencement of the College of St. James, Wednesday, July 11th, 1860*, Subject file, "Education--St. James's College," MDA; *Register of the College of St. James, 1858*, 22.

[71] WWD to ABD, 25 November 1860, ABD Letters.

out of your mind. Yesterday and last night we had, decidedly, the coldest weather we have had this year. This morning I hear the ice is strong enough to bear a person.

I suppose you will begin to think about killing hogs, pretty soon, if the weather continues in this way. Please let me know how large a pen you have, and how you think they will turn out.

Ma wrote me word several weeks ago that you thought of selling Ashland. I should like very much to know what you have done with it. I dont think you would make a very bad bargain even if you parted with it at a sacrafice.

I hope you and Ma will not be too sanguine in your hopes of my taking a second testimonial. Since I have commenced Greek I have given up all hopes of taking it, for in this study I cannot get good marks, although I study it quite as hard if not harder than any other member of the class. The spare time too which I had hoped to spend in reviewing, in order to pass a creditable examination at Christmas, has all to be given up to Greek and Mathematics, and I have sometimes to spend a good part of my recreation hours on them.

Dr. Kerfoot appears to have been very much pleased with his visit to Montgomery. He said he had a very pleasant time.

Give my love to Ma

>   Your devoted Son
>   W. W. Davis

P.S. Since writing the above I have been over to Dr. Kerfoot's study. He spoke of his visit to Greenwood, and expressed himself very much pleased with it and its inhabitants, and Dr. K. is a man who generally means what he says. Dr. K. is about to establish a Sunday school for the children in the neighborhood, and spoke to me about becoming a teacher. Nothing could give me more pleasure than this if I thought I could do any good, if any teachings of mine could open the way for the light of the everlasting gospel, to some poor benighted soul. Although this will be a poor recompense for all the good things God has given me, still I feel that it will make me more acceptable in his sight. I think I will try and see what I can do asking his divine mercy and guidance for Christ's sake.

>   Your affectionate son,
>   W. W. Davis

W. Wilkins Davis to Rebecca Dorsey Davis[72]

St. James College
Decem. 5th 1860

Dear Sister,

I received your letter last night, and feeling somewhat unwell to day I thought I would let my lessons slide, and employ myself in answering it. Last Thanksgiving day I was appointed to fill the vacancy at the head of the third prep. table which appointment I have held ever since. I am by this appointment made a kind of prefect, having to care for, and at the same time to keep in order a dozen of the smallest,--but-- decidedly the most mischevous boys at the college. You may imagine what a nice time I must have! I am unable to read at table, for it is a perfect bedlam, and I am continually employed in trying to keep my unruly crew in something like order. I, however make the waiter bring me coffee for tea, which I would not otherwise get.

Congress has at last met and the great problem will soon, I have no doubt be solved, whether this grand experiment of Republican government shall, or shall not succeed. I think the political demagogues of the South must have employed a Rhetorical artifice known as "diversion of feelings" in order to

---

[72] WWD to RDD, 5 December 1860, ABD Letters.

stir up such vehement indignation against the perpetuation of the Union. They have by high flown panegyrics on Southern rights, and vague declamations of Northern aggression, associating with them a host of stimulating ideas, charmed the minds of the ignorant and unthinking, and raised such a tumult of feeling as has effectually blinded their judgment. When men come to consider carefully the expediency of the projected step, men both North and South will be found a little too selfish, calmly and indifferently to hazard the great blessings they now enjoy, their dearest hopes for the accomplishment of an end so trivial.

    Give my love to Ester and Marrie
      Your devoted brother
       W. W. Davis

W. Wilkins Davis to Allen Bowie Davis[73]

      St. James College
      Decem. 9th. 1860

Dear Pa,

  I can scarcely realize the fact, that Christmas is but two short weeks off. The two months since I left home have flown

---

[73] WWD to ABD, 9 December 1860, ABD Letters.

by with fearful rapidity. I have, generally, heard it said that the longer any person remains away from home the less he cares for it, but my experience has failed to verify this. The trite old saying that "There is no place like home," has to me at present just as much reality as it had six years ago when I first went to boarding school. Old Greenwood, and all the fond recolections that cluster arround it, are as near, and as dear to me as ever and the affection that I have always felt for that dear old spot is deepened by the thought that twelve months hence, instead of hailing the natal day of our blessed Redeemer with carols and joyous anthems, with a thankful remembrance of the great blessings we enjoy, we may be called upon to mourn over the broken and dishonored fragments of our glorious Union.

Can it be that northern men are so blind as calmly and indifferently to sacrafice their dearest interest for the attainment of an end so trivial? and can it be that southern men have been so carried away by high flown panegyrics on state's rights, and vague declamations on northern aggression, as to allow their better judgement to be so utterly perverted. Ambition, blind ambition, and party strife; these it was that undermined the liberties of Greece, of lovely Greece the cradle of art, of literature and of science, the land of the poet and the sculptor, long since passed away and forgotten; to these too is repubblican Rome indebted for her downfall; and these it is, that are gnawing at the vitals of our dear fatherland. Sad it will be if this gorgeous fabric, which we received so pure and unsullied from the hands of our ancestors, is to melt away like some beautiful myth, and if the United States of America is destined to become a by-word and a scoff among the nations of the earth.

> Give my love to Ma.
> Your devoted son
> W. W. Davis

Hester Ann Davis recorded similar fears in her diary on Christmas Day. "A heavy pall of darkness hangs over our future," she wrote. "Where will we be next Christmas.... Shall we enjoy the comforts of a Greenwood fireside or shall we be compelled to fly for our lives, and to find security in the City." Her sympathies at this time lay with the South: "If the North refuse to redress our grievances, we are pledged to unite with the South and withdraw from the Union. If the North refuse to allow us peaceably to secede, than Civil war with all its horrors must ensue. Oh heavenly father we beseech thee to have mercy on us...."[74]

On 8 January 1861 William A. Muhlenberg wrote his friend John Kerfoot and offered his opinion on the crisis at hand: "There are mad people on both sides, but it is not any

---

[74] HAD diary, 25 December 1860.

Northern madness which now makes the trouble, but the deliberate and determined sentiment of the North in regard to slavery, which the South will not endure. That cannot be changed. In any rupture of the Union, Maryland will sooner or later be found with the free States. St. James's may suffer for awhile, but will be found in a good position ultimately."[75] Of course the last prediction turned out to be incorrect; the College very shortly found itself in desperate circumstances with a fraction of the student body it accommodated in normal times. And the first part of 1861 marked the beginning of Wilkins Davis's decline also, as he contracted the first of a series of illnesses that would eventually force him to quit the College of St. James and to search in vain for a restoration of his health in Minnesota.

---

[75] Muhlenberg to Kerfoot, 8 January 1861, in Harrison, *Life of Kerfoot* 1:149-50.

W. Wilkins Davis to Rebecca Doresy Davis[76]

St James College
Jan. 10th. 1861

Dear Sister,

I have forgotten which one of you wrote to me last, but thinking it would not make much diference to which one I wrote, I thought I would scribble off a few lines to you.

I suppose you are all by this time safely lodged at Ingleside, and I have settled down for a pretty tough siege untill Easter.

I suppose you have heard by this time that reinforcements have been sent to Charleston. The steamer Star of the West left New York on Monday with 250 soldiers on board, and a stock of provision for fort Sumpter. We had no news from Charleston yesterday, and it is suposed that the South Carolina authorities have prohibited all telegraphic communication with the United States government. It was rumored in yesterdays papers, that the Charleston batteries had opened fire on the Star of the West and that Major Anderson had, in consequence, commenced to bombard the city. Although this is but a rumor, and could be traced to no

---
[76]WWD to RDD, 10 January 1861, ABD Letters.

reliable authority, I fear it will prove too true, and if such should be the case, then, in my humble opinion, the doom of our glorious Union is, irrevocably, sealed. God grant I may hold a wrong opinion.[77] I had great confidence in the religious observance of the fourth, but the dark and threatening news of the last two nights has entirely obliterated the delusive phantom of hope to which I have been clinging.[78] Whether the people of this land were too far gone in sin and wickedness to humble themselves before the throne of the Almighty, or whether the national sins of which we have been guilty were too monstrous for so meagre an atonement I know not and it is not for man to seek to pry into the secret decrees of the Good God, but I am thoroughly convinced that no human aid can save us, and we have only to look to Him from whom all good things come and submit ourselves to his divine commands.

   Give my love to Ester and Marie.

      Your affectionate brother,

       W. W. Davis

---

[77] The merchant ship *Star of the West* approached Charleston harbor on 9 January with 250 troops aboard. It was fired upon before reaching Fort Sumter, whereupon the ship retreated and headed back to New York. Major Robert A. Anderson, commander of U.S. forces at Fort Sumter, decided not to return the fire opened on the relief vessel. On 13 April Anderson finally had to surrender the Federal garrison to Confederate officers. By this time no food and an insufficient number of men remained and further resistance was deemed useless.

[78] Friday, 4 January 1861, had been set apart by President James Buchanan as a day of "humiliation, fasting, and prayer throughout the Union." *The American Annual Cyclopedia and Register of Important Events of the Year 1861* (New York, 1862), 294.

On 19 January Hester Ann Davis wrote in her diary her views on secession and the Union: Regarding the southern leaders "I say be not joined unto them. I am afraid of them. They have not sufficient <u>Wisdom</u> and discretion to construct a new government. Before I can consent to pulling down our glorious Union I must be very sure one more permanent is to be reared in its stead. I want to live and die in the 'United States of America,' and have as the flag of my nation ... the <u>star spangled banner</u>. The people in the South, are deluded and ruled by ambitious politicians, and artful demagogues."[79] The next day she said in a letter to Wilkins that "Your father recieved a letter this afternoon informing us of your illness. I felt too thankful when the letter wound up by saying you were out of danger and indeed almost well. I hope you will be careful of yourself as it might have been Pneumonia, or Inflammatory rheumatism, both dangerous diseases at this season, a relapse often proving fatal." She then passed along some somber news: "I was reading yesterday that one fourth of the human race die under seven years, another fourth under seventeen years, you have safely passed those stages, but death the reaper has put in his sickle and will soon gather all his harvest home. 'Be wise to day! Tis madness to defer.' Both you and I may be in the next sheaf." She bade him seek Christ

---

[79] HAD diary, 19 January 1861.

and pray for change so that his heart would not be tempted by earthly things.[80]

In the same letter she remarked that Mr. Seward "certainly missed a grand opportunity for merging the politician in the great statesman. He said the country must be saved and would be saved by the people. He was willing for this, that, and the other when a direct expression of his willingness to compromise on the <u>Territorial</u>, would almost have settled the matter." What Hester Ann Davis was referring to was an important speech made in the United States Senate on 12 January by William Henry Seward, who would shortly become secretary of state in the Lincoln administration. By this time Mississippi, Florida, and Alabama had followed South Carolina out of the Union. Two thousand men and women packed the Senate galleries to hear Seward's comments and proposals. His patriotic call for renewed efforts to preserve the Union was eloquent and moving, but many of those who heard him or who read his remarks, like Hester Ann Davis, found him hazy on specifics and ambiguous as to his actual intentions. The contents of his speech admitted a wide range of interpretations. Of course this was a large part of Seward's purpose. The leading Republican proponent of a policy known as "voluntary reconstruction," Seward believed that if Republicans refrained from provocative acts against the seceded states and even offered some timely concessions, the

---

[80] HAD to WWD, 20 January 1861, ABD Letters.

upper South would remain loyal and the lower South would eventually rejoin the Union. Consequently, he said he was willing to see all personal liberty laws repealed, he would back a constitutional amendment forbidding forever to Congress the power to abolish or interfere with slavery in any state, and he would support a proposal to admit New Mexico (which included what is now Ariziona) as a state. The last item amounted to an apparent violation of the Republican platform because slavery was legal in the territory, but Lincoln reluctantly approved the proposal because he was confident slavery could never take root in the area. Several southern congressmen saw Seward's plan as a trick to split off the upper from the lower South by the mere appearance of granting concessions. They and three-quarters of the Republicans voted against it; the House finally rejected the measure in March.[81]

On Sunday, 27 January, Hester Ann Davis commented in her diary that Seward spoke of how the Union had to be saved but in fact did nothing. She also wrote of her son's health: "Wilkins has been ill, for five days could not turn over in bed, or lift his head from his pillow. I feel very uneasy about him." In the following letter, written while Wilkins was sick at St. James's, a "Dr. Dorsey" is mentioned. Frederick Dorsey, M.D., of Hagerstown, had been a strong supporter of the College of St. James, serving it from its inception as trustee,

---
[81] HAD to WWD, 20 January 1861, ABD Letters; Glyndon G. Van Dusen, *William Henry Seward* (New York, 1967), 244-46; McPherson, 138-39.

physician, and benefactor. But he died, at the age of 84, in 1858. The doctor who attended Wilkins must, therefore, have been either his son, John Claggett Dorsey (1805-1863), or his grandson, Frederick Dorsey (1834-1888). Both son and grandson were medical doctors who had shared a practice with the elder Dorsey until his death; both served at the time of Wilkins's illness as school physicians at the College of St. James. It is interesting to note that the first Dr. Dorsey was well known for favoring blood-letting and the purgatives jalap and calomel as remedies for a variety of afflictions.[82]

W. Wilkins Davis to Hester Ann Davis[83]

St. James College
January 27th/60 [1861]

Dear Ma,

I received your letter last night. The eatables have not yet arrived, but I suppose I will get them pretty soon. I think I told you in my last letter that I had been out riding. My feet got very cold and the day after I had a relapse. It was not near

---

[82] *Register of the College of St. James, 1860*, 39; Scharf, *History of Western Maryland* 2:1134-38; Williams, 265-66, 270.

[83] WWD to HAD, 27 January [1861], ABD Letters.

so serious as the first attack. The doctor bled me pretty freely and applied hot mustard poultices to my left side, where I suffered most pain, and I was soon relieved. My side is still so sore that I am not able to sit up much, and I cant do anything but stay pened up in this little room, which is 10 x 13 feet, all day long. I have been sick for two weeks and have only been outside of this room twice the whole time.

I dont believe I would weigh much over a hundred pound now,[84] I have fallen off so much. The doctor, Dr. Kerfoot and all agree that I want rich nourishing food, but I dont see much of it. They got me some oysters, but they were spoilt and I had to throw them away, they also gave me chicken several times but it was so tough I could not eat it. They pay such poor prices here for everything that the neighbors wont bring any but the poorest things. If Dr. Kerfoot did not stick so close to Dr. Dorsey when he comes out, I think I would suggest to him that a change would be beneficial to me, but he wont give me a chance. I hope I'll soon be able to get out of this place, for I am awful tired of it.

        Give my love to Pa
        Your devoted son
        W.W. Davis

---

[84] By this time Wilkins stood close to six feet, three inches in height. HAD diary, 26 December 1860.

[Attached to the same letter are the following two paragraphs by Hester Ann Davis:]

Wednesday afternoon

Dr Husband

    I enclose you Wilkins letters. It demands your serious consideration. I fear his constitution may recieve a vital stab by so many relapses and such severe remedies. Suppose you go up their Saturday and bring him down Monday. I could send over the close carriage to the cars. He ought not to venture out in an open vehicle of any kind for fear of another relapse. Something must be done and done quickly. He is our only son, almost our only Earthly hope and his health should engage our utmost care....

Affectionately yours
H A Davis

I am very much alarmed about Wilkins. It may result in a Confirmed pulmonary affection. You had better go up. Perhaps you could go Friday, and come down Saturday by the afternoon train and I send over the carriage. I fear the Rockaway would be too open.

Wilkins did come home to Greenwood and slowly regained his health; at least he grew well enough to return to the College--in March or April--and complete the junior year, his last at the school. During this period of recuperation he was treated by Dr. Augustus Riggs (1803-1873) of Cooksville (a village nine miles north of Greenwood) and possibly also by his brother, Dr. Artemas Riggs (1814-1884), whose office was in Brookeville.[85] For several days after Wilkins's arrival at Greenwood he remained, in his mother's words, "very feeble," though he was still strong enough at first to sit "in a rocking chair reading by the kerosene a 'very superior novel.'"[86] A fortnight into his stay at home he was unable to manage even that. Hester Ann Davis wrote to Esther on 20 February that

> Your poor brother's rheumatism still hangs on. He is confined to his bed, yesterday a blister was put on his side; this morning the pain in his side and oppressed breathing is relieved, but great tenderness continues. Dr. Riggs from Cooksville ... thinks the heavy dose of Calomel and jalop, and the antimony powders, reduced his system, and relaxed his muscles; in that state the exposure to a damp atmosphere brought on

---

[85] John Beverly Riggs, *The Riggs Family of Maryland* (Baltimore, 1939), 413-16; HAD diary, 26 [February] 1861; HAD to EWD, 20 February 1861, ABD Letters.

[86] HAD to daughter, 5 February 1861, ABD Letters.

114

inflammatory rheumatism, a disease by the by to which the Bowie family are predisposed.[87]

Meanwhile, the sectional crisis grew steadily worse. Hester Ann Davis feared that when the Lincoln administration took over the government on 4 March, it would try to enforce "certain government laws in the Southern states" and that this action would lead to resistance and civil war.[88] "We are at present," she said, "like a ship becalmed in a heavy fog, no sun, no moon, no stars to be seen above our horizon."[89] At the College of St. James Kerfoot estimated hopefully that three-quarters of the southern students were pro-Union; but as a precaution to prevent discord and distractions from the tasks at hand, he asked all the boys to refrain from giving speeches or writing essays on political topics.[90] Hester Ann Davis believed that if the constitutional amendment that had just been approved (on 28 February) by the House of Representatives--one preventing the Federal government for all future time from interfering with slavery in the states--was passed by the Senate as well, Maryland would be "safe," that is, would remain in the Union. "I have always been a free soiler," she wrote in her diary, and "[would never vote for the extension of slavery]

---

[87] HAD to EWD, 20 February 1861, ABD Letters.

[88] HAD to daughter, 5 February 1861, ABD Letters.

[89] HAD to EWD, 20 February 1861, ABD Letters.

[90] Harrison, *Life of Kerfoot* 1:199-200.

unless to save the Union. As a domestic institution it is a <u>state right</u>, with which Congress has no right to interfere; but as 'might is right' seems to be the creed of the majority, It is but right the border states should have such a guarantee." The amendment she spoke of was in fact passed by both houses of Congress, but these votes were of little consequence; the proposed amendment failed to be ratified by more than two states, Ohio and Maryland, before the war began. In time a very different Thirteenth Amendment--one abolishing slavery-- became part of the U.S. Constitution.[91]

On 16 April Allen Bowie Davis wrote Wilkins, who had returned to the College of St. James, and told him of his deep regret that "our beloved Country is now involved in Civil War, the most horrible of all national contests." He feared the next point of attack would be Washington, D.C. "Should the result of all this trouble involve us in ... civil strife, anarchy and rebellion it may be that you will have to come home to aid in protecting and defending our own neighborhood or to protect and defend the Capital of our country." He added that "it is a great misfortune that we have at such a time a president for whom we cannot entertain political sympathy and hardly personal respect--it greatly weakens the chances of sustaining the Government. I think a Marylander should if possible keep out of the contest, but this may not be practicable." He asked

---

[91]HAD diary, 2 March 1861; Catton, 197-98; McPherson, 136; Nevins, *The Emergence of Lincoln: Prologue to Civil War 1859-1861*, vol. 4 of *The Ordeal of the Union* (New York, 1950), 409-10.

Wilkins not "to become too much excited upon the subject so as to let it interfere with your studies and the advantages you <u>now</u> have, for the opportunity may never return to you again.... I hope your health continues good so that you are able to study well so as to regain some of your lost time."[92] One day later Hester Ann Davis wrote her daughters--who were all now at Ingleside--and commented upon the "difference of opinion in our state, some for upholding the present government, others for joining the Southern Confederacy. I believe the majority are for the Union but all opposed to war.... Washington is strongly guarded, and the most fearful excitement prevails every where."[93]

In another letter to her daughters Hester Ann Davis spoke of the war in apocalyptic terms:

> Can it be possible that we are living in the last days of the present dispensation? Wars, rumors of wars, earthquakes, pestilences, famines, nation rising against nation, kingdom against kingdom.... It is believed the 7th and last vial has just been poured out and we are entering upon such troubles as never have been witnessed on earth before.... You may live to see the descent of the Messiah and the restoration of the Jews, or the abolition of slavery, or the destruction of the

---

[92] ABD to WWD, 16 April 1861, ABD Letters.

[93] HAD to daughters, 17 April 1861, ABD Letters.

present order of things. I have been reading Cumming he cites a host of commentators who fix it in 1867. So like Job in my flesh I may see God.

The author Mrs. Davis had been reading was undoubtedly the Reverend John Cumming (1807-1881). He had published a series of popular works with such titles as *Apocalyptic Sketches, Prophetic Studies, The Coming Wars...*, and *The End; or, The Proximate Signs of the Close of This Dispensation.*[94]

On 14 May, Allen Bowie Davis summed up recent events in a letter to his daughter Rebecca. "I am glad that Maryland is still in the Union--it would be utter ... devastation for her to attempt to seeed. The South could not protect her and she would be a prey to the northern hordes. The Legislature has adjourned because they found they could not take her out...."[95]

In the letter below Wilkins proclaims himself "a straight out 'Southern Rights' man." Kerfoot observed in the spring of 1861 that, indeed, "the hottest talkers [for secession] for months had been young Marylanders, all sons of Union men! Each of them I saw privately and gave them the option of abstinence from debates that excite, or a return at once to their

---

[94] HAD to daughters, 20 April 1861, ABD Letters.

[95] ABD to RDD, 14 May [1861], ABD Letters.

fathers."[96] Bowie Davis's son was probably one of those students the rector had in mind. Wilkins wrote this letter and his next one during the first period of concerted military activity in the vicinity of St. James's. The most important nearby site was Harpers Ferry, about twenty miles south of the school. Strategically located at the confluence of the Shenandoah and Potomac rivers, it was considered the key to the Shenandoah Valley. The town was a major arms-producing center and, because of the Baltimore and Ohio Railroad and the Chesapeake and Ohio Canal, a vital link between the East and the Ohio Valley. It changed hands a number of times during the Civil War. By the beginning of May four thousand Virginians occupied Harpers Ferry; an equal number of Federal troops were encamped in Chambersburg, Pennsylvania. On Sundays Marylanders who were southern sympathizers would visit the Confederate camp, while Union supporters rode out to see the Federals in Chambersburg. Some young men from Washington County joined the Confederate army at Harpers Ferry.[97] On 9 May CSA General Thomas J. Jackson occupied the Maryland Heights--a ridge opposite Harpers Ferry--with Kentucky and Virginia troops. By 20 May a thousand Confederate troops were encamped on the Potomac River opposite Williamsport, a Maryland town only four miles northwest of the College of St. James. In late May and early June over ten thousand U.S. troops were

---

[96] Kerfoot to Whittingham, 19 June 1861, in Harrison, *Life of Kerfoot* 1:215.

[97] Williams, 308.

concentrated in Chambersburg preparatory to a Union effort to retake Harpers Ferry.[98]

W. Wilkins Davis to Rebecca Dorsey Davis[99]

St. Jas. College
May 22d. 1861.

Dear Sister,

I received your most welcome letter yesterday evening.

For your benefit I hereby announce myself, henceforth, a straight out "Southern Rights" man, and want nothing to do with Lincoln, his party, or anything connected with him, or it, unless it is to help to thrash him. I remained by the Union as long as I could, but when I saw it was the intention of Lincoln and his crew to convert into a despotism, the freest, and best goverment ever instituted by mortal man, I concluded that the sooner I shook off all allegiance with him, and everything connected with him, the better. I can no longer support a man

---

[98] Williams, 309; Maryland Civil War Centennial Commission, *Maryland Remembers: A Guide to the Historic Places and People of the Civil War in Maryland* (Hagerstown, MD, 1961), 47; Scharf, *History of Western Maryland* 1:213.

[99] WWD to RDD, 22 May 1861, ABD Letters.

whose avowed intention is to subjugate the South. The very act of trampling upon, and treading in the dust the most sacred rights guaranteed to all the states, alike, in the Constitution, converts the government into a despotism, justifies revolution, and renders the duty of defending their rights and vindicating their honor imperative on the Southerners. And so I am henceforth for the "Southern confederacy," and the right.

If you could only see the tyrannical way in which "Abe" wields his despotic sceptre over Maryland, and the insults he has offered, and continues to offer to her, I think your Union, or rather ExUnion proclivities would be a little weakened. And our contemptible, cowardly, lying governor winks at every thing [he] does without the least compunction.

We are beginning to be pretty lively up in this part of the world. An advanced guard of 1500 Virginians has encamped within four miles of us, at Williamsport, and we are daily expecting the advance guard of 10,000 Pennsylvanians at Hagerstown six miles on the other side of us. Just between the two fires we may have the pleasure of seeing a battle if not of participating in it. Good number of our students have visited the Virginia camp, but lynx eyed John B. [Kerfoot] got wind of it and made us a stump speech on the subject last night. He said he had his spies out and that he would ship, otherwise, dismiss all students he caught in the direction of Williamsport. We will be able to see the smoke and hear the firing when they get to fighting at Harpers Ferry, and at night we will be able to see the bombshell flying from the Maryland heights batteries.

> Give my love to Ester and Marrie
> Your devoted brother
> W. W. Davis

Wilkins's mother was not happy about her son's new political opinions. She told Rebecca "I hope your brother will escape this <u>strange delusion</u>. We may not like the present administration, nor endorse its acts--but--'we had better bear the ills we have than fly to others that we know not of.' Let Maryland remain neutral and she may ride out safely this awful storm. Oh if I only could feel sure she would--but I fear this secession element. It would be certain ruin to all <u>our hopes as a family</u>, in this world."[100]

Wilkins wrote at least two other letters during this period of late May and early June that are now lost. His father reacted to them in a letter in which he told Wilkins he appreciated his "sound advice" on a real estated transaction he was contemplating, but that he could not

---

[100] HAD to RDD, 24 May 1861, ABD Letters.

express the same satisfaction with regard to the political sentiments you write to your mother. I very much fear that the vague and captivating sound and clamor for "Southern rights" and the well founded prejudice against Lincon who for the time being unfortunately happens to be the President of the nation has mislead your judgment. I very much fear, and shall be greatly deceived if the sequel does not prove that the means now taken in the South to secure "Southern rights" in lieu of the protection secured by the laws and the Constitution, does not prove the complete destruction of Southern rights if not of Constitutional liberty. Before I can adopt the heresy of Secession as a remedy for Southern wrongs, I must ignore the teachings of Washington, Jefferson, Jackson, Monroe, Adams, Clay, Webster, and even Calhoun himself, with almost every other leading statesman who has preceeded our times. And if the theory be right in it self, it is passing strange that it should require so much fraud violence and usurpation to adopt and sustain it."

Davis believed that had it not been for Lincoln's election secession would not have found political support "outside the aristocratic ... State of South Carolina, whose excitable French blood will perhaps for generations to come keep her in a continual state of discontent, if not of open revolt. I pray you my dear Son to exercise your natural calmness and judgment in looking at this subject. You already see enough to see how utterly impracticable and ruinous it would be for Maryland to join the Southern Confederacy--to her it would be ... destruction." In a postscript Allen Bowie Davis passionately defended his commitments, indeed his whole life, against his son's suggestion that he and his wife took the political positon they did out of a narrow concern for their own material welfare.

> In your letter to your Ma you speak of sacrificing "honor to interest." The enquiry at once arises, what interest have we heretofore enjoyed which has so suddenly become dishonorable in your eyes? Is it the love and affection with which I have clung to the house of my fathers, and devoted all my life to beautify and improve to make it dear to my children. Is it the proud satisfaction I have felt that my lot and that of my children to come after me, was cast, as it were, directly under the shadow of the Capitol, grand in all its recollections and ample proportions and ornaments, natural and artificial? Is it that the loyalty, patriotism love of Union and Maryland as one of first and most devoted members of the Union has been all along living in dishonor? For the life of me I cannot feel or see the dishonor we have been so long living in and which we are now suddenly called upon to cast off as filthy rags ... because interest must be sacrificed to honor. If my lot and calling is an honorable one then it becomes

dishonorable to sacrifice it to even a sense of honor. How are the two incompatible?[101]

Wilkins wrote the following letter just as Union troops were on the move from Chambersburg to Harpers Ferry by way of Hagerstown and its environs. Another U.S. force was marching up the northern bank of the Potomac from the District of Columbia toward the same site.

W. Wilkins Davis to Rebecca Dorsey Davis[102]

St. James College
June 12th/ 61

Dear Sister,

I received your most welcome letter last evening. You need not worry yourself about sending me strawberries, for I stowed away enough, at dinner to day, to last me a week. We have had them twice this year, and expect to have them a couple of more times.

---

[101] ABD to WWD, 4 June 1861, ABD Letters.

[102] WWD to RDD, 12 June 1861, ABD Letters.

We have more Ex United States troops arround us now than we can shake a stick at. We have been laughing, for the last twenty four hours, over the milk and water attempt of that time serving old tody, Gov. Hicks, to get himself out of the scrape, into which he got himself, by letting such an egregious falsehood about the bridges.[103]

As my class is about to be broken up, we have determined to exchange photographs with each other according to custom. We will go into Hagerstown to have them taken as soon as the excitement occasioned by the troops being there dies out a little. As it will, in all probability, be the last time I will ever have the pleasure of visiting Hagerstown, I think I will have to call at Mrs Romans. Sally will be home in about a week, but if I should go in before then, I guess I'll have to call on the mother.[104] They have invited me there several

---

[103] Hicks claimed that at the meeting on the evening of 19 April he had said he had no authority to give his consent to the burning of the bridges, that the proposed act was unlawful, that he was a lover of law and order, and that the mayor could do as he pleased. Hagerstown *Herald of Freedom and Torch Light*, 19 June 1861.

[104] The mother referred to was Louisa Margaret Kennedy Roman, wife of James Dixon Roman (1809-1867), a prominent Hagerstown lawyer and political figure. Mr. Roman was a member of the U.S. House of Representatives in the late 1840s and a member of the Peace Conference that met in February 1861. Sallie Roman (1843-1873) became the wife of Columbus C. Baldwin, a wealthy New Yorker originally from Maryland. After fire destroyed St. John's Church in Hagerstown in 1871 a new church was built, the spire and stone tower of which were given by Baldwin in memory of his late wife; in the tower he caused a peal of bells to be placed as a special tribute to her. The former rector of St. John's and a man integral to the founding of the College of St. James, Theodore Lyman, attended the

times to spend my hollidays, but I never even called to see them, so I think it would be about as little as I could do to go and bid them good bye. I have some idea of going into the apothecary business next year, in order to study Chemistry and Materia Medica practically, preparitory to my commencing the study of Medicine regularly.

>Give my love to Ester and Marrie
>Your devoted brother
>W. W. Davis

Let me know when
you are going home.

Union troops reached Hagerstown on 15 June. The local newspaper described the excitment in the city caused by the sight of bristling bayonets and the sound of the "stirring notes of the drum and fife." Within a few days 15,000 Federals passed through Hagerstown and the county.[105] Four thousand of these troops spent the night of 15 June in a large field just south of the College of St. James after mistaking it for their

---

opening services in the new church building in 1875 as bishop of North Carolina. Williams, 307, 379, 381-82; Scharf, *History of Western Maryland* 2:1180.

[105] Hagerstown *Herald of Freedom and Torch Light*, 19 June 1861; Nevins, *The War for the Union: The Improvised War*, 158.

assigned location. Students mixed with soldiers, and, according to Kerfoot, "all went on cheerfully." A moment of tension did occur when several of the soldiers asked in threatening tones why no U.S. flag was flying over the school; apparently some of the boys had been spreading rumors that the College was "secession." A flag was found and put up forthwith. Fitz-John Porter happened to be with these troops serving as adjutant general under the commanding officer, Major General Robert Patterson; the son of the College matron proved helpful in acting as a liaison between Kerfoot and the military authorities.[106] As the Union troops approached Harpers Ferry, the Confederates, under General Joseph E. Johnston, abandoned the Maryland Heights, where they had some artillery mounted, and fell back to the main body on the Virginia side of the Potomac River. On 15 June Harpers Ferry itself was evacuated; the southern troops retreated to a more defensible position near Winchester, Virginia. Before they quit the area, engineers from General T. J. Jackson's force blew up the 1000-foot-long B. & O. railroad bridge that linked Harpers Ferry to Maryland.[107]

---

[106] Kerfoot, as quoted in Harrison, *Life of Kerfoot* 1:212-14; Williams, 311-12, 314. For an account of Porter's career see Otto Eisenschiml, *The Celebrated Case of Fitz John Porter* (Indianapolis, 1950).

[107] McPherson, 159; Scharf, *History of Western Maryland* 1:214; Daniel Carroll Toomey, *The Civil War in Maryland* (Baltimore, 1983), 23; Hagerstown *Herald of Freedom and Torch Light*, 19 June 1861; Catton, 443. It will be recalled that Patterson's activity in the period following his repossession of Harpers Ferry formed an important part of a larger series of events that together constituted the prelude to the first major engagement of the Civil War, at Bull Run. The failure of Patterson's force to prevent the

On 27 June Rebecca Davis wrote her brother and urged him to "try and study up for the examinations and dismiss politics awhile. I have come to the conclusion that the least said on the subject is decidedly the happier way; for the discussing of it causes such disagreeable felings." To underscore her point Sister Beck sent along a poem she had written:

> Ma's grieving over her prodigal son,
> And longing for his safe return,
> She hopes the fatted calf to kill
> When she shall change his iron will,
> She knows he loves her glorious flag
> More than an old secession rag,
> Will wave and wave o'er the land of the brave
> When secession's dead and in its grave.[108]

Confederate army under General Joseph E. Johnston from uniting with General Pierre G. T. Beauregard's men at Manassas Junction was a significant factor in the defeat of General Irvin McDowell and his army of raw, undisciplined troops.

[108] RDD to WWD, 27 June 1861, ABD Letters.

Wilkins's Later Career and Death

Whether Wilkins ever sloughed off his pro-South attitude is unknown because he did not discuss his political beliefs in any of his later letters. If he did hold on to them he undoubtedly found the anti-Lincoln views held by many of those on the faculty of the University of Maryland's medical school, which he attended in the fall of 1861, much to his liking. All that is known about the period he spent studying medicine is what is contained in two items, a letter to one of his sisters and a printed card admitting him to a series of lectures. He wrote Rebecca on 27 October that he had attended fifteen or twenty lectures, read books on chemistry and anatomy, and "been in Dr. Smith's office."[109] Nathan Ryno Smith (1797-1877) held the chair of surgery at Maryland for fifty years. He was a strong southern sympathizer (he even enjoyed writing romantic essays about plantation life) as well as a renowned physician. As a surgeon he was confident, imaginative, and--this was especially important in the days before anesthesia--swift. Once a week students watched him carry out impressive feats in the operating theater; at other times they followed him on his rounds to see the results of his work. Wilkins undoubtedly found him a redoubtable and inspiring figure. The other item in the Allen Bowie Davis Letters is a small printed card that reads "University of Maryland/lectures on/Materia Medica and General

---

[109] WWD to RDD, 27 October 1861, ABD Letters.

Therapeutics,/by Samuel Chew, M.D./Session of 1861-62/Admit Mr. W. W. Davis." Wilkins's name has been filled in in ink on the last line. Dr. Chew (1805-1863) was professor of the principles and practice of medicine at Maryland.[110]

In 1862, when Wilkins suffered another affliction on the lungs, he withdrew from his medical studies and acted on the advice of those who told him he stood his best chance of regaining his health if he escaped the moist air of Maryland and took refuge in a state with a dry, fortifying climate. In November, supplied with a letter of introduction to Bishop Henry Benjamin Whipple (1822-1901) and accompanied by his cousin Washington ("Wat") Bowie III (1841-1922), he journeyed to Minnesota.[111] By Christmas he had made contact with the bishop and was on his way to becoming a beloved member of the Whipple household.[112] Indeed, in a letter to his

---

[110] Printed card, ABD Letters; Eugene Fauntleroy Cordell, *The Medical Annals of Maryland, 1799-1899* (Baltimore, 1903), 818-35; idem, *Historical Sketch of the University of Maryland* (Baltimore, 1891), 63; Calcott, 117, 154; Scharf, *History of Baltimore City and County*, 754.

[111] Washington Bowie Memoirs, Minnesota Historical Society, St. Paul (photostat). Washington Bowie III was the son of Catherine Worthington Davis and Thomas Johns Bowie. He stood out in his family as an ardent Democrat and as an active supporter of the South during the Civil War. After the war he served on the staff of Governor Oden Bowie and as an official of the Port of Baltimore. Farquhar, *Old Homes and History*, 276; Bowie, 217.

[112] A similar course was followed by the Reverend Leonard J. Mills, an 1858 graduate of the College of St. James and a former tutor there of Latin and Greek. Because of poor health, he left his parish in Prince George's County, Maryland, in September 1865 and went out to Minnesota. He, too, was

Reprinted from Whipple, *Lights and Shadows of a Long Episcopate*, frontispiece.

Henry Benjamin Whipple

mother he mentioned that on Christmas Day the bishop had given him "a beautiful little pocket prayer book" and that other members of the family had also given him presents. He closed this letter by saying "Farewell my dear Mother. I know that your prayers will accompany me in my journey through the wild wastes of this far off western land, and trust that a kind providence will save and protect me from harm and enable me speedily to return in health and strength to the enjoyment of the pleasures and comforts of home--sweet home."[113]

Wilkins was occupied during much of his time in Minnesota as an assistant to Bishop Whipple, helping him with correspondence and travelling with him all over that vast region. In letters home he described his trips, solicited funds for missions ("many a time have I seen the Bishop take the money, that he could ill spare, out of his own pocket to keep his missionaries from want"), and spoke of his increasing physical vigor.[114] On 2 December 1863 he wrote his mother that "I came here as a stranger and a wanderer and he took me into

---

assisted by Whipple, who appointed him chaplain of the new diocean school for girls, St. Mary's Hall, in Faribault. Mills died, probably of tuberculosis, in 1866, only six months after entering upon his new work. Vertical file, MDA; George Clinton Tanner, *Fifty Years of Church Work in the Diocese of Minnesota 1857-1907* (St. Paul, 1909), 234, 414-15; Henry Benjamin Whipple, *Lights and Shadows of a Long Episcopate* (London, 1899), 189.

[113] WWD to HAD, 25 December 1862, ABD Letters.

[114] WWD to sister, 21 June, 2, 5, 22, 26 December 1863, ABD Letters. The quotation is from the letter of 5 December 1863. RDD diary, 8, 15, 22, 29 August, 12, 26 September, 17 December 1863, MS. 2111, MHS.

the bosom of his family and watched over me with the tender care and love of a father and by his great care and kindness restored me from an almost hopeless invalid to a state of comparative health." He said he treasured the Whipple family second only to his own kin and would remember his days at the bishop's residence in Faribault as among the happiest of his life. He indicated he would like to buy a farm, seeing such a venture as "the best thing I can do to ensure a return of my health." He could not help feeling discouraged at times, though:

> I know it is wrong for me to give way to such feelings but there are few who so early in life have had the misfortune to meet with so many disappointments and when I look back upon the many fond hopes crushed and the airy castles I was wont to build fading one by one away I cant but feel sad. I will try however to shake off this feeling and look forward with hope and confidence that all will come out right in the future-- submitting cheerfully to whatever chastisement my Heavenly Father may see fit to inflict, comforting myself with the assurance that there is not one unnecessary drop in the bitter cup which he presents to me.

He told his mother he would not consider "marrying early"; not only was his health too precarious for such a step but he was unwilling to subject a woman he loved to the "hardships and trials" of Minnesota. But, he said, "I candidly confess to you that my heart is not as free as it was when I wrote to you on the subject last spring."[115] Bishop Whipple wrote to Allen Bowie Davis in the fall of 1863 and told him he and his family had learned to love Wilkins too much to let him leave them and that Wilkins ought to remain with him as travelling companion through the winter; after that, if his health was good, he might engage in an occupation of his own.[116]

Wilkins visited Greenwood for five weeks in the summer of 1864. He appeared well and strong and again spoke of his desire to buy a farm. Rebecca noted that "he is much attached to Mrs. W. Miss Nellie and indeed the whole family; is treated as though he was one of them and enjoys all the family secrets." By September Wilkins did own a farm, one purchased for him by his father and located about three miles outside of Faribault.[117] Apparently, though, even after he entered upon this new arrangement, he continued, on occasion at least, to assist Bishop Whipple.[118] He still spent every Christmas with the Whipple family. In April of 1865 he told

---

[115] WWD to HAD, 2 December 1863, ABD Letters.

[116] RDD diary, 24 October 1863.

[117] RDD diary, 4 July, 10 September 1864; Roger Brooke Farquhar, "Honorable Allen Bowie Davis of Greenwood...," [August 1, 1930], C. A. Porter Hopkins Papers, MS. 2005.1, MHS.

[118] He continued to handle some of the bishop's correspondence, for instance, in Whipple's absence. WWD to Clark W. Thompson, 22 September 1864, Clark W. Thompson Papers, Minnesota Historical Society (photostat).

his father in a letter that he was now "quite set up in the Insurance business."[119] It is doubtful, however, that Wilkins was able to become truly established in any line of work before his final illness struck in December of 1865.

Wilkins's relationship with the Whipples established a lasting bond between the two families. On the bishop's visits to Washington to see Lincoln or Grant or whoever he thought might be able to improve the lot of the Indians, he frequently stayed at Greenwood.[120] At the Davis home, he said, "I ... found a quiet resting-place ..., where the old traditions of Southern hospitality were kept up."[121] He made one such visit in April 1864, accompanied by the Reverend Samuel D. Hinman, a missionary to the Dakotas; Enmegahbowh (the Reverend John Johnson), an Ottawa Indian and a missionary to the Ojibway; and three Dakotas, Pay-Pay, Taopi, and George St. Clair. Mary Dorsey Davis observed that the day Bishop Whipple preached, "the church at Mechanicsville was crowded to overflowing," and everyone "seemed delighted with [him]." One person who heard him commented that if the bishop were there on a regular basis everyone would join the

---

[119] WWD to ABD, 2 April 1865, ABD Letters.

[120] For a brief introduction to the career of Bishop Whipple as a reformer of U.S. policy toward the Indians, see Martin N. Zanger, "'Straight Tongue's Heathen Wards': Bishop Whipple and the Episcopal Mission to the Chippewas," in *Churchmen and the Western Indians*, ed. Clyde A. Milner II and Floyd A. O'Neil (Norman, OK, 1985), 177-214.

[121] Whipple, 315-16.

Episcopal church. And "Ma says the Bishop is elegant and was born to be a Bishop. I think he is one of the few saints that dwell upon the earth."[122]

On 20 December 1865 Wilkins wrote to one of his sisters--probably Rebecca--just as he was beginning to wage his final bout with consumption: "This is a hard country to be sick in at any time, but when the thermometer goes down to 30 below zero, its terrible."[123] When the gravity of his condition became clear to members of his family back home, Rebecca was chosen to go out to this forbidding environment to try to bring her brother some cheer; Wat Bowie also went out to be with his cousin.

Two others who regularly looked after Wilkins during his final weeks were Bishop Whipple's daughter Cornelia ("Nellie") and the Whipples' physician, Jared Waldo Daniels. Cornelia Ward Whipple was born in Adams, New York, on 26 August 1845. She and Wilkins were married on 22 February

---

[122] MDD to RDD, 11 April 1864, ABD Papers, Box 1. Whipple made this trip in the spring of 1864 in order to induce Federal officials to do three things: reconsider a treaty the government had negotiated fraudulently in 1863 with the Red Lake and Pembina Ojibway; give the Dakotas, who had been exiled from Minnesota as a result of the 1862 Dakota Outbreak, a decent place to live; and provide restitution of some sort to the Dakotas-- including Pay-Pay, Taopi, and George St. Clair--who had been friendly to the whites during the outbreak but nonetheless suffered the same fate as the hostiles, losing thier land and their annuities. Letter received from Jean Haskell, 9 July 1987.

[123] WWD to sister, 20 December 1865, ABD Letters.

1866, only a week before he died. Of course it was clear at the time that Wilkins would shortly succumb to his illness. The *Montgomery County Sentinel* said of this last major act of Wilkins's life that "It was a beautiful and touching exemplification of our friend's real character, that, when he became assured that his life was rapidly ebbing away, he requested to be joined, in holy wedlock, to her whom he had hoped to lead to the altar under happier auspices--that he might, at least, bequeath to her the right to mourn for him."[124] Because of his love for Nellie, his gratitude to her, and his concern for her future, Wilkins may have wanted to bequeath to her greater means and independence as well; through marriage he brought Nellie into his own family and assured her a portion of his inheritance. Of course this act was also a way of expressing his love for his adopted family and of assisting them, too. In 1875 Nellie married Francis Marion Rose, a Faribault physician. She died of consumption on 21 May 1884.[125] Dr. Daniels (1827-1904) practiced medicine in St. Peter and Faribault but also devoted much of his career to working among the Indians. He was government physician to the Sioux in 1860 and, later, agent at the Sisseton Reservation in what is now South Dakota and at Red Cloud in Nebraska. He assisted

---

[124] *Montgomery County Sentinel*, 6 April 1866 (microfilm, Montgomery County Public Library, Rockville).

[125] Nellie was survived by her husband and by a son, Francis Marion Rose Jr., born 4 July 1881. Letter received from Jean Haskell, 9 July 1987; Charles H. Whipple, comp., *Genealogy of the Whipple, Wright, Wager, Ward, Pell, McLean, Burnet Families* (n.p., 1971), 21.

Bishop Whipple in providing emergency relief to the Sissetons and Wahpetons in 1868-1870 and served with Whipple on the 1876 Sioux Commission. He treated members of the Whipple family and was named the first school physician for St. Mary's Hall, the bishop's school for girls in Faribault.[126]

In his 20 December 1865 letter, the last piece of his correspondence that is extant, Wilkins mentions Nellie, Dr. Daniels, and others and describes his diet:

> Miss Nellie drove me out this morning for a little ride. Dr. Daniels thinks I am decidedly better this morning, and with care will pick up quite rapidly. I was doing very nicely about ten days ago, but got chilled ... which brought on a little relapse. Dr. Daniels is a very cheerful and pleasant man, and attended me very faithfully. I think his coming when he did was providential for me--for if I had been left without medical attention I am afraid you would have had a sad Xmas. I am beginning to look for Wat Bowie.... I really need him the next few weeks very much.... I can never be too grateful to Mrs. Whipple and Miss Nellie for their kind attentions to me. The bulk of my diet at present is Egg nogg and beef tea--Egg nogg I guess a little different from your style--two eggs yellows and

---

[126] Letter received from Jean Haskell, 2 June 1987; Whipple, 285, 286, 293, 298, 300, 301, 302.

whites beat up separately, two tablespoonfuls of milk a little sugar and a tablespoonful of brandy--this dose I worry down before I am out of bed every morning. The Drs object is to get me to take a couple of raw eggs every day. I still continue my 3 lbs of beef tea and all I feel like eating besides--which dont amount to a great deal. Miss Nellie sends her love.[127]

In early February 1866 it looked as though Wilkins was getting better. Rebecca was now with him. Allen Bowie Davis wrote her to say recent news from Minnesota had been encouraging to the whole family: "his continued improvement is most cheering and fills us with gratitude to a kind Providence that has enabled you to reach him--and him to be so far improved as to enjoy your Society, and be cheered and comforted by your presence."[128] Over the next few weeks, however, Wilkins's condition worsened. On 2 March Mr. Davis, staying at his winter residence in Baltimore, received a telegram from Wat Bowie in Faribault: "Wilkins failing very fast free from pain and perfectly resigned." The next day Wat sent his uncle another message: "Wilkins quietly fell asleep in Jesus at six last Evening."[129] Allen Bowie Davis received further information about his son's last moments in a letter

---

[127] WWD to sister, 20 December 1865, ABD Letters.

[128] ABD to RDD, 3 February 1866, ABD Letters.

[129] Washington Bowie III to ABD, telegrams, 2,3 March 1866, ABD Papers, Box 1.

from his nephew: "He was perfectly calm quiet and resigned, passed away without a struggle--like an angel going to sleep. Certainly a purer spirit never soared to Heaven, and Heaven never received a more Christian Soul." No one, Wat said, "ever had more friends, none ever won more hearts.... My dear cousins Rebecca and Nellie bear it as well as could be expected. Wilkins had a devoted wife, and a devoted sister." Wat said he would make the arrangements for having the body shipped home. He mentioned that Dr. Daniels had "been like a Father to Wilkins, watching him closely, he has always alleviated his sufferings."[130]

Bishop Whipple travelled to Maryland with members of his family and gave the address at Wilkins's funeral. He said "I have never been called to bury one where it was so hard to say, 'farewell'--and I am sure never where there was so little cause for tears." He characterized Wilkins as a gentle and faithful young man, well liked by everyone: "He ... left friends at every missionary station in my Diocese." And the bishop spoke of Wilkins as his valued co-worker: "He has been my companion in missionary journeys, and no one in my diocese has shared as he, every joy and sorrow of my heart. I told him as I thought to myself of all my plans for Christian work, and I always found in

---

[130] Washington Bowie III to ABD, 2 March 1866, ABD Letters.

the sympathy of his young heart strength for the roughest and the hardest trials of a border-bishop's life."[131]

Wilkins's body was buried at Greenwood in the family cemetery. The spot where he and his parents and sisters lie is marked by a white marble shaft, ten or twelve feet in height, topped by a carved urn with a shroud. Allen Bowie Davis gave a stained-glass window at St. John's Church, Mechanicsville, as a memorial to his son. It depicts St. John the Evangelist and stood for many years above the altar; in 1980, when the church was enlarged, the window was relocated to the west transept, where it may be seen today. When Allen Bowie Davis died in 1889 he left $300 in his will to establish a fund for the upkeep of the church, particularly the chancel, wherein "I have erected a memorial window to my deceased son William Wilkins Davis."[132] When Mary Dorsey Davis died in 1939, at the age of 93, she left to St. John's Church the family cemetery and $1500 for its maintenance.[133] The Davises' relations with the Whipple family and others in Minnesota continued after Wilkins's death. Bishop Whipple travelled to Maryland in 1888 to give the address at Hester Ann Davis's funeral. Rebecca began

---

[131] ABD to William Rollinson Whittingham, 12 March 1866, MDA; *In Memory of Wm. Wilkins Davis ... Funeral Address by Right Rev. H.B. Whipple ...* (Baltimore, 1866), 3, 4.

[132] ABD will, ABD Papers, Box 1.

[133] Parish records, "Memorials and Gifts 1842-1984," St. John's Church, Olney, MD.

while her brother was alive to collect money from her friends to send to Bishop Whipple to support his mission work.[134] Throughout the 1870s and '80s she corresponded with Enmegahbowh and sent him contributions of money and clothing; he in turn wrote her of his family and of his activities at the White Earth Reservation.[135] In her will Rebecca left $100 to "my friend, Rev. Wilkins Davis Smith, Indian Deacon, Waytahevansh, Minn."[136]

---

[134] RDD diary, 4 July 1864.

[135] J. J. Enmegahbowh to RDD, 12 February 1877, 25 November 1878, 12 January 1883, 7 January 1885, 28 July 1890, Lucy Leigh Bowie Collection, MS. 1755, Box 2, MHS.

[136] RDD will, ABD Papers, Box 1. It was common practice for Whipple and other missionaries to give the names of their own relatives and friends to the Indians they baptized. This particular Indian's identity and place of residence are both mysteries. No such place as Waytahevansh is known to have existed. The will in the ABD Papers is an unsigned, typescript copy; it is possible that RDD wrote out the correct name in her own original draft--perhaps Nay-tah-waush, which was a village on the White Earth Reservation--and it was subsequently copied incorrectly by the typist. Another Indian who bore Wilkins's name was William Wilkins Davis Pakinemawash, baptized by Whipple in 1863. H. B. Whipple journal, 25 October 1863, Diocese of Minnesota Papers, Box 42, Minnesota Historical Society. This Indian may have been the Christianized Ojibway known as Pay-kin-a-waush, who moved to the White Earth Reservation after it opened to the Ojibway in 1868. Letter received from Jean Haskell, 29 July 1987.

III
CONCLUSION

The letters of W. Wilkins Davis do not contain any dramatic new revelations about the College of St. James. The program of study, the regulations, the prizes, the literary societies, the chapel services--all these ingredients of life at the school that Wilkins mentions were already well known through other sources. Nor do his letters include any piquant gossip or depictions of the seamier side of student life. There is no hint in them of sexual scandal or even of violence (except against some hapless animal subjects). The reader may even miss the stories of drinking and fighting and whoring that may be found in accounts of the English public schools. True, Wilkins may not have wanted to confess his or his comrades' more outrageous sins to his pious parents or his strait-laced sister, but one perceives through reading these letters that the College of St. James really was a thoroughly different place from Shrewsbury or Eton or Charterhouse in the 1850s. The boys at St. James's led closely supervised, highly regulated lives in a rural location six miles from the nearest town. They lacked the tradition of rebellion and much of the opportunity for wild behavior available to their British counterparts. They were all younger brothers in a patriarchal household whose *raison d'être* was the training of boys' minds, souls, and bodies according to Christian principles. What Wilkins's letters reveal that official publications cannot is that this controlled environment, reinforced by the family at home, did have an effect. The sort of cynicism that an Etonian or Harrovian of this period would have expressed toward his school's chapel and curriculum is not present in Wilkins's letters, save in regard to the College's food.[1]

These letters, then, portray a small institution largely achieving its purpose in an isolated setting in the Maryland countryside. But of course the picture they paint is more complicated than that: crowding into the scene are images of strife and disintegration; the men and materiel of battle are already visible along with other signs that things are about to fall apart. Today's observer makes out what is there on the canvas but can also see what lies just beyond the frame: the collapse of the College of St. James at about the same time that William Tecumseh Sherman was converting the larger struggle into total war, Wilkins succumbing to the tubercle bacillus, the traditional way of life of the Indian coming under assault in the West, the comfortable synthesis of religious and scientific truth elaborated by men like Charles Bell on the verge of being dissolved by Darwinism.

---

[1] For an excellent acccount of the British schools see John Chandos, *Boys Together: English Public Schools 1800-1864* (New Haven, 1984).

The College of St. James was a vital school for many years but it lacked the resources to meet the trauma of sectional conflict: it did not have the wherewithal to move to its alternative site in Baltimore County; it did not even have the capacity to allow its students to debate the subjects of secession and lawful coercion.[2] The College was simply overwhelmed by the inexorable process of civil strife. Not long after Wilkins penned his last letter from St. James's, nearby cornfields were trampled under foot by thousands of young men no older than he, sunken roads were turned into bloody lanes, and Marylanders who had hoped to avoid war found themselves forced to undergo a fiery trial.

---

[2] Of course Kerfoot's immediate aim in banning political debate was to preserve the harmony and safety of the school, but it is worth noting that by the time of the rector's order Episcopal Church leaders had built up a long tradition of avoiding discussion of controversial political questions (such as slavery). They had sought to prevent discord within the church by maintaining a firm boundary between matters of church and matters of state. During the Civil War this tradition of political noninvolvement came to an end. See Mullin, 124-30, 198-211.

www.ingramcontent.com/pod-product-compliance
Lightning Source LLC
Chambersburg PA
CBHW072144160426
43197CB00012B/2245